100 Ideas for
Early Years Practitioners

Outdoor Play

Other titles in the 100 ideas for Early Years Practitioners series:

100 ideas for Early Years Practitioners: Outstanding Practice by Lucy Peet

100 ideas for Early Years Practitioners: School Readiness by Clare Ford

Other titles in the 100 ideas for Primary Teachers series:

100 ideas for Primary Teachers: Behaviour Management by Molly Potter

100 ideas for Primary Teachers: Dyslexia by Gavin Reid and Shannon Green

100 ideas for Primary Teachers: Developing Thinking Skills by Steve Bowkett

100 ideas for Primary Teachers: Outstanding Teaching by Stephen Lockyer

100 Ideas for Early Years Practitioners

Outdoor Play

Julie Mountain

B L O O M S B U R Y

LONDON • NEW DELHI • NEW YORK • SYDNEY

Bloomsbury Education

An imprint of Bloomsbury Publishing Plc

50 Bedford Square	1385 Broadway
London	New York
WC1B 3DP	NY 10018
UK	USA

www.bloomsbury.com

Bloomsbury is a registered trade mark of Bloomsbury Publishing Plc

First published 2015

British Library Cataloguing-in-Publication Data
A catalogue record for this book is available from the British Library.

ISBN: PB: 9781472911032
ePub: 9781472911056
ePDF: 9781472911049

Library of Congress Cataloguing-in-Publication Data
A catalog record for this book is available from the Library of Congress.

10 9 8 7 6 5 4 3 2 1

Typeset by Newgen Knowledge Works (P) Ltd., Chennai, India
Printed by CPI Group (UK) Ltd, Croydon, CR0 4YY

This book is produced using paper that is made from wood grown
in managed, sustainable forests. It is natural, renewable and
recyclable. The logging and manufacturing processes conform
to the environmental regulations of the country of origin.

To view more of our titles please visit www.bloomsbury.com

Contents

Acknowledgements

Writing a book is an enormous privilege, but it can't be done alone. My sincerest thanks go to the countless teachers, practitioners and colleagues whose joy of and commitment to outdoor play has inspired me over the years. In particular I'd like to thank Gail Ryder Richardson and Jan White who never fail to question and challenge my thinking, Ruth Barker for kicking off my own passion for outdoor learning and play and my mum for making me 'go out and play!' in every kind of weather.

'Thank you and sorry' to my ever patient family – Matt, Olly and Ted – for putting up with me disappearing to 'do some book' whenever anything needed doing around the house...

I'm hugely grateful to my 'guest' authors for sharing their inventive ideas and I hope to return the favour one day:

Idea 7: The quote at the start of this idea is from the Community Playthings website. Download a free PDF of their wonderful block play booklet *I made a unicorn* from: www.communityplaythings.co.uk

Idea 8: Thanks to Kierna Corr, nursery teacher and outdoor play blogger at Learning for Life, for sharing this idea. nosuchthingasbadweather.blogspot.co.uk

Idea 12: This idea is inspired by the work of Sue Humphries and Susan Rowe at the Coombes Primary School, Berkshire. From *The Coombes Approach*, Bloomsbury Publishing Plc.

Ideas 13, 50 and 94: Thanks to Felicity Robinson, early childhood landscape specialist at Play Learning Life, for sharing these ideas. www.playlearninglife.org.uk

Idea 22: With thanks to Jan White and Muddy Faces for the mud kitchen ideas and inspiration. www.muddyfaces.co.uk

Idea 25: Thanks to Lesley Romanoff, Bottle baby pioneer at Takoma Park Cooperative Nursery School, Maryland, for sharing this idea. www.takomacooperativeschool.org

Idea 27: Thanks to Lily Horseman of Kindling, a playwork and Forest School provider, for sharing this idea. Discover more of Lily's fabulous ideas by following Kindling on Facebook (www.facebook.com/kindling1) and Twitter.

Idea 31: With thanks to members of the Forest Education Initiative Facebook group for generously sharing their quirky suggestions. http://tinyurl.com/foresteducation

Ideas 42 and 95: Thanks to Juliet Robertson, outdoor learning champion and award-winning education blogger, for sharing these ideas. www.creativestarlearning.co.uk

Ideas 44, 45, 46, 89 and 92: Thanks to Mary Jackson, teacher and outdoor learning specialist at Play Learning Life, for sharing these ideas. www.playlearninglife.org.uk

Introduction

Your role as a practitioner is crucial in unlocking the potential of the outdoors. Your knowledge and experience, your understanding of each child's needs and your willingness to embrace new approaches to learning means that the special nature of outdoors can be an integral part of early childhood for every child, regardless of age, ability or cultural context.

Outdoors is special – and it is different from indoors. Harnessing the pleasures and treasures of outdoor play ought not to be daunting, but it often is. Lack of time, space, or resources, the weather, parent attitudes and staff ratios are all cited as reasons for keeping children cooped up indoors, when the evidence suggests they would much rather be learning and playing outdoors and would benefit in a whole range of ways if they were spending more time outdoors.

The unique features of the outdoors suit the learning styles of young children. Outdoors, they can move, make noise and use their bodies in big, exuberant ways. Children's imperative to know why things happen can be met in the most memorable way: through first-hand testing in an environment that lends itself to lively science and problem solving.

The incredible developmental journey of young children places intellectual, emotional and physical demands on them. Outdoors, these demands are met through different types of active, collaborative, thought-provoking and purposeful play:

- open-ended play, in which children are able to shape the outcomes
- manipulative play, through which muscle groups build strength and coordination and the brain makes new connections
- physically-challenging play, where resilience and persistence are tested and nurtured
- cognitive and imaginative play, with friends or in peaceful, solitary nooks helps children make sense of their experiences and the world around them.

This book aims to be a springboard to outdoor play. It contains ideas for meaningful outdoor activities for every day of the week, no matter what the weather and whatever the range of abilities in your group. The book starts with Part 1 – a section called **Firm foundations** which is intended to provide an introduction to the principles and practicalities that enable high-quality outdoor play to take place. The rest of the book is split into the following parts:

- **Brilliantly simple starters** are quick and easy outdoor activities that require minimal preparation or equipment.
- **Enabling environments** examines the role of outdoor features and facilities in enabling and sustaining high-quality outdoor play.
- **Naturally playful** contains ideas that make the most of the changing seasons, natural materials and the weather.
- **Inspiring outdoors** is about creativity outdoors and includes suggestions for art, music, dance, storytelling and installations.
- **Take a risk!** focuses on more challenging and thrilling activities, which require preparation and robust 'risk benefit' assessment procedures.
- **Whatever the weather** will help ensure there is exhilarating outdoor play, every day of the year.
- **Scientists and engineers** recognises children as instinctive explorers and inventors, and suggests ways of helping them test and challenge their curiosity.
- **Playing out counts** aims to help children make sense of early maths concepts through playful outdoor activities.
- **Up and at 'em!** contains physically demanding activities that support all areas of young children's early development.
- **Speak out** completes the book with ideas that celebrate children's emerging communication skills and makes the most of the outdoors as a stimulus for talk.

The ideas in this book have been tried and tested and are easily adapted to suit the needs of any young child. Many of the activities require minimal preparation and all of them reflect the budget constraints common in most settings. The highest quality outdoor play is not about expensive resources and it's certainly not about fixed play equipment or endless seas of garish rubber flooring. It's not even about plants, trees and flowers (although access to nature really does have a genuine impact on outcomes for children). It's about you and the children making the most of what you have and expressing willingness to share what you know.

Outdoors, children feel freer. They recognise and appreciate the freedom to move, talk, shout, leap, hide, climb, whizz and breathe. Outdoors, children are excited to 'show and tell' and they'll share their time and their treasures generously. The best way for you to harness the special nature of the outdoors is to get out there too, to share your time and your treasures with the small people in your care. Enjoy!

How to use this book

This book includes quick, easy, practical ideas for you to dip in and out of, to help you plan your outdoor learning.

Each idea includes:

- A catchy title, easy to refer to and share with your colleagues.
- An inspirational quote, or a quote from a teacher or student describing their experiences of the idea that follows or a problem they may have had that using the idea solves.
- A summary of the idea in bold, making it easy to flick through the book and identify an idea you want to use at a glance.
- A step-by-step guide to implementing the idea.

Each idea also includes one or more of the following:

Teaching tip

Some extra advice on how or how not to run the activity or put the strategy into practice.

Taking it further

Ideas and advice for how to extend the idea or develop it further.

Bonus idea ★

There are 36 bonus ideas in this book that are extra exciting and extra original.

Involving parents

Tips for how to get parents and carers involved in their children's learning.

Share how you use these ideas and find out what other teachers have done using **#100ideas**.

Firm foundations

Part 1

Vision and values for outdoor play

"Knowledgeable and enthusiastic adults are crucial to unlocking the potential of the outdoors."

Led by Jan White and Learning through Landscapes, a group of 30 leading organisations, academics and practitioners came together to formulate a 'Shared Vision and Values' document to encapsulate the essential outdoor experiences every child should have. This guidance now underpins the approach of many practitioners working with young children outdoors.

Involving parents

Communicating a vision for outdoor play to parents is vital – parents should also be 'knowledgeable and enthusiastic adults' and can play their own crucial role in supporting high quality outdoor play. Plan an open day (see Idea 4), send out newsletters, annotate photo-stories on the setting's website and talk to parents at pick up time, focusing on what outdoor play did for their child today.

Three points make up the vision statement:

- All children have the right to experience and enjoy the essential and special nature of being outdoors.
- Young children thrive and their minds and bodies develop best when they have free access to stimulating outdoor environments for learning through play and real experiences.
- Knowledgeable and enthusiastic adults are crucial to unlocking the potential of the outdoors.

There are also ten principles, known as the 'values' and you can read the full text of them on a downloadable poster at tinyurl.com/EYvision. These values include commentary about outdoor play having purpose and meaning for young children and being rooted in real life experiences. They also introduce the concept of the 'special nature' of outdoors. Outdoor play is not the same as indoor play and it's not appropriate to simply bring indoor play outdoors. Play and learning outdoors should reflect the unique features of outdoors, complementing, extending and enriching indoor provision.

Throughout the values narrative, the role of the adult is emphasised and this is also highlighted in one of the three guiding vision statements. Without adults who want to be outdoors, who are properly resourced to be outdoors and who understand children's fascination with outdoors, the potential for the outdoors to support and scaffold, excite and motivate, nurture and reward will be missed. Adult commitment to purposeful outdoor play is essential.

Research into outdoor play in young children suggests that they see outdoors as 'their' domain, with indoors being very much controlled and managed by adults. Outdoors, children are able to control and shape their play – there's more space and more resources, they can make noise, they can hide away, get messy and watch the world go by. Outdoor play offers the freedom that many children crave. It's important when you plan your outdoor time and space that you focus on child-led opportunities and ensure children have lots of time to explore and to return to follow their interests.

Taking it further

Why not use a staff meeting to think about what *your* setting considers to be elemental about outdoor play? Consider questions such as: what should every child in our setting be able to do outdoors? What's unique about our outdoor space? Why is outdoor play so essential for young children? Use your answers to these questions to create your own bold vision statement for outdoor play – and remember to share it with parents.

Bonus idea

Explore what other organisations and settings say about outdoor play. An Internet search using the terms 'outdoor play policy' or 'early years outdoor play' will highlight dozens of examples of inspirational vision and policy statements, practical ideas and case studies.

Planning safe outdoor play

"No child will learn about risk if they are wrapped in cotton wool."
Health and Safety Executive

In an increasingly sedentary and risk averse society, the outdoor play spaces at early years settings take on even greater importance; where else can young children learn to manage risk, explore the natural and man-made world at first hand and test what their bodies and minds can achieve . . . and still be 'as safe as necessary'?

Involving parents

Appreciating the value of outdoor play is just the start; sharing it is key to improving outcomes for children. The significance of a play-based curriculum is not always widely understood by parents, and outdoor play can often be the contentious element that prevents innovation. Parents who don't understand how their child benefits from freely chosen, open-ended play with natural materials will find the grazes, muddy knees and dirty clothes difficult to accept. This will inevitably become apparent to their children, who will then be less willing to engage in active outdoor play. Communicating the joy and value of outdoor play and the purpose of enabling risky and challenging play in the lives of children will help overcome these barriers. See Idea 49, Outdoor gallery, for more inspiration.

The pre-school garden is a safe, managed environment – certainly compared to most parks or gardens. Your features and activities are risk assessed, your colleagues are knowledgeable and experienced, and children are helped to play together, share resources and listen to instructions. You have a head start. However, providing challenging, risky activities – which some of the activities in this book are – can be daunting.

Risk benefit assessment is an approach to risk assessment that focuses on *enabling* an activity to take place, rather than preventing it. It starts with the premise that the activity is valuable, beneficial and worth doing; these benefits are listed *before* the hazards are examined. The remainder of the approach is similar to a standard risk assessment: identify the potential hazards, describe how they could be mitigated and decide what the overall risk rating then is.

This approach is now recommended by Government departments, Play England and the Play Safety Forum. Even the Health and Safety Executive recognises the importance of enabling children to take risks, stating that:

Play is great for children's well-being and development. When planning and providing play opportunities, the goal is not to eliminate risk, but to weigh up the risks and benefits. No child will learn about risk if they are wrapped in cotton wool. (Health and Safety Executive Children's Play and Leisure – Promoting a Balanced Approach, September 2012: www.tinyurl.com/HSEplay)

Dynamic risk assessment is a fundamental part of staying safe outdoors and application of common sense is the guiding principle. Be aware of the potential risks involved in children's play but equally, be realistic about the likelihood of the risk and the severity of the consequences. If the risk of injury is negligible – and it often is – and the consequences are acceptable, then you should enable children to take risks, not prevent them. See Idea 53, You learn to fall by falling, for more details.

Taking it further

Observation and assessment are often overlooked outdoors. If we value the skills and attributes children develop outdoors then we need to document this and analyse the outcomes as closely as we do for indoor learning. For some children, the learning they do outdoors is the most meaningful and the most memorable. It's therefore vital that the evolution of these skills and attributes is recognised, and the resources, places and activities that stimulate learning most effectively are recorded to enable dissemination and provide evidence of progress. Adapt (if necessary) your setting's standard observation and evaluation template to ensure it captures children's learning through play outdoors.

Outdoor play policy

"Playing out is essential and a right for every child."

An outdoor play policy demonstrates a strong statement of intent to parents, staff and potential funders. It shows that you are committed to children's right to play outdoors and can provide a richly resourced, appropriately supported enabling play environment. If you don't have an outdoor play policy already, create one over the course of two or three staff meeting sessions.

Start with a short, focused statement that encapsulates your approach to outdoor play. Then use these discussion points to help you write a policy:

- What do we believe children are entitled to in terms of outdoor play?
- How do we support and develop our staff to ensure they are enthusiastic and knowledgeable outdoor practitioners?
- What steps do we take to ensure our resources and equipment are in good condition and fit for purpose?
- How does a sustainable world come into our outdoor play policy?
- How do we communicate the importance of outdoor play to our parents?
- How do we include outdoor play in children's learning journey documentation?
- What is our attitude to risky and challenging outdoor play?
- How does outdoor play develop independence, resilience and responsibility in our children?
- Do we use a risk benefit approach to risk assessment? See Idea 53, You learn to fall by falling, for more information about this approach.

Doing this demonstrates to staff your commitment to their professional development in this area. It's important that parents know the policy exists and how it shapes your outdoor play.

Outdoor play open day

"Helping parents understand the true value of outdoor play was the single most effective action we took in our bid to improve the quality of outdoor play."

Sometimes, the biggest barrier to better outdoor play is parents' attitudes; if they don't value outdoor play then they won't understand why their children are out in all weathers, come home scuffed and mucky and haven't spent the day at a desk. Help parents to see the value of outdoor play by organising an open day.

After you have circulated an outdoor play policy, organise an outdoor play open day for parents. The open day actually only needs to be a couple of hours for parents to drop in.

- Focus on high quality play outdoors, providing resources that demonstrate strong curriculum links and enabling children to take responsibility and make choices.
- Ask staff to be Outdoor Play Champions, chatting with parents and discussing the value of outdoor play, the importance of risk and challenge (See Idea 53, You learn to fall by falling) and the opportunities and resources at your setting.
- Encourage parents to observe the children at play, only intervening if invited to do so by children. Ask them to look out for ways that children communicate with one another, how they think creatively and express themselves – help parents see how the curriculum's requirements are fully met through outdoor play.
- Discuss each child's outdoor play preferences with their parents. Focus on the areas of development in which they excel outdoors (for example, imaginative play) and talk about how parents can help children reach other developmental milestones by planning more outdoor play at home.

Teaching tip

To encourage parents to attend organise refreshments – including hot drinks if it's a chilly day!

Taking it further

Invite a group of current and prospective children and parents to attend the setting on a Saturday morning and allow them to explore your garden, experiment with resources and play freely outdoors. Ask your local paper to come along to talk to parents and children – it's a great opportunity to position your setting as an outdoor play specialist.

Super storage

"When it comes to storage, one size most definitely does NOT fit all!"

Storage is one of the most troublesome issues for settings — and yet, it needn't be. You find yourself worrying about the size, the location, the cost, the accessibility, the inaccessibility . . . but the trick is to think about what you actually need, rather than what you think you want.

Making the right decisions about storage is vital. Get it wrong and you'll be cursing for years. Get it right and you'll be amazed at how much less setting up and packing away there is for you, and how much more independent your children are.

- Start by making an inventory of everything you use outdoors. This means *everything* — not just the resources that live outdoors, but also the items you bring from indoors to use outdoors. It can help to use a spreadsheet for this, or make a list on a large piece of paper.
- Next to each resource, indicate whether you are happy for it to be independently accessed by children (C) or only accessed by adults (A). Think carefully about this — do all the items marked A really need to be adult access only? What would the risk be if children were able to access them? What would the benefits be?
- Now add an initial or acronym to identify where the resource is generally used — zone your outdoor space into logical areas, for example garden, bike track, sandpit, bushes, climbing area. If the item is used everywhere, mark it with 'All'.
- Now add a note to indicate whether each item requires lots of storage space (for example, bikes), little space (for example, skipping ropes) or is a 'grab and go' type resource box (for example, digging tools).

Several different types of storage are almost always better than one large shed.

- Low-level, shallow, front opening units are great for 'grab and go' boxes and other small items you are happy for children to access independently, such as chalk and hula hoops.
- A long, low shed works well for wheely toys – it doesn't need to be tall, just lofty enough to allow children to park their vehicles in their 'garage'.
- A hefty shed can store large independently accessible items (for example, bikes and trikes, or hollow blocks) on its floor; smaller, independently accessible resources in storage containers on low shelves and items you'd rather manage the use of (for example, Forest School resources) on higher shelves.
- Use large hooks on the doors, walls and ceilings to store hoops, wet weather gear, gardening tools and bags of resources.
- Research storage options online. Most shed manufacturers will customise storage to your specific requirements and it's not always wildly expensive. Look at what other settings have done by searching Pinterest, or other online 'pinboards'.

Involving parents

A storage revamp is a great way to involve parents in the practicalities of outdoor play. Invite parents to assist with annual inventories, quality checking, relabelling containers and, of course, fundraising to purchase new storage units or containers. Consider a special one-off fundraising event such as a quiz, a September welcome barbecue or a music evening. These events often raise sufficient funding to provide a new shed, or dozens of high quality, robust, stackable and (best of all!) matching storage containers.

Affordances and loose parts

"We were able to 'see' our space with fresh eyes and begin to understand where children's inspiration for play came from."

Affordance theory, developed by psychologist JJ Gibson, proposes that objects have multiple uses, which depend on both the environment they're in and the way the objects are perceived by people. Architect Simon Nicholson's loose parts theory has been equally influential in shaping how we provide for play.

The theories of loose parts and affordances provide insight into how children play and how we can resource a space to add richness and diversity to their play.

JJ Gibson suggested that babies and young children understand affordances of objects before they know what objects actually are and make use of objects they come across, regardless of the original purpose. 'The affordance of an object is what the infant begins by noticing. The meaning is observed before the substance and surface.'

Open-ended resources are rich in affordances; simple objects such as buckets and sticks, natural materials such as sand and mud and imported items such as tyres and crates are abundant in affordances and will be used in a multitude of ways by innovative, questioning children.

The theory of loose parts suggests that children gain value from play with objects that can be moved, transported, manipulated, combined and organised in dozens of previously untested ways. Loose parts items can be natural (conkers) or man-made (hollow blocks) and can be tiny (marbles, shells) or hefty (tyres, crates). What they have in common is that none of them have a clearly defined use or predetermined outcome.

Brilliantly simple
starters

Part 2

Brilliant blocks

"We use hollow blocks in my school every day and I always tell people that they are the most open-ended and cost-effective resource you can buy – they never wear out." Community Playthings

Modular hollow blocks are an early years outdoor play essential. Whilst they can be pricey, they represent excellent play value, as most loose parts resources do. Moving, stacking and ordering the blocks promotes agility and coordination along with collaboration and communication skills.

Teaching tip

Always store hollow blocks under cover – whilst they are robust, if constantly exposed to damp, they will eventually become slippery.

Taking it further

Add natural materials to a hollow block play scenario, for example baskets of conkers, acorns, sets of straight sticks, a trug full of crunchy dry leaves or shells. Be generous and abundant with the resources!

Make the most of blocks with the following activities:

- **Shark infested waters:** Can children arrange the blocks so that it is possible to get from one end of the garden to the other without stepping on the ground?
- **Volcano:** Show children footage of erupting volcanoes and ask them to combine blocks and crates to build their own volcano. A few pieces of red or orange fabric could become the lava.
- **Bridge building:** Experiment with risky play by building bridges, beginning with a single block high and working upwards, adding extra blocks or differently shaped blocks. Test each bridge – what changes to the design do children need to make to create a stable bridge? What precautions should they take to keep themselves safe on the bridge?
- **Make music:** Set up a range of different size and shaped blocks like a giant drum kit, stacking some of them two or three high. Use percussion beaters, sticks or hands to beat out rhythms. Does each block make the same sound? What about if they are stacked? Which 'beater' is the best?

Crate fun!

"Working together, the boys built a volcano, four crates high!"

Props for good-quality outdoor play don't have to be expensive. Children can turn everyday objects into anything they need them to be at that time — thrones, beds, steps, suitcases ... The possibilities for play with a milk or bread crate are endless in the hands of an imaginative child.

Crates are open-ended, versatile objects that can be used for a variety of purposes. Best of all, they can be left outside all year round with no fear of them becoming rusty or getting ruined by the elements.

- Ask a friendly milk delivery service, a bakery or a local supermarket if they are willing to give you a few spare crates.
- Crates can be stacked when not in use or left around the space to be used as informal seating.
- When not in use, crates can be used as an extra storage item for outside toys, sticks or balls etc.
- Crates are light enough for young children to move around freely and yet, because of their size and awkwardness, they still provide enough of a physical challenge to give those large muscle groups a workout.
- Crates are great for giving children a little more independence in order to access items that are normally hard to reach.
- In a waterlogged garden or through mud, crates can provide a useful dry walkway, keeping children off soggy grass.

By Kierna Corr

Teaching tip

Encourage children to move the crates around the space as much as possible, but have a 'resting' place for them to be returned to at the end of each play session.

Taking it further

Create elaborate walkways out of crates for the children to discover when they arrive. They could wind around the space and lead to key features. Watch how children interact with the walkway to see what works and what does not. Tell children there are sharks in the water encouraging everyone to climb up and down again!

Walking on the Moon

"Walking on the Moon is a great way to encourage children to stretch and jump, carefully and slowly, around the objects in our garden."

Changing the shape, volume or centre of gravity of our bodies alters the way we move and makes even the most familiar tasks more difficult, requiring concentration and determination. Help your children refine their balance and coordination by giving them 'Moon feet'.

Show children images or a YouTube video of astronauts walking on the Moon or undertaking space walks from the International Space Station. Talk about the awkward spacesuits the astronauts are wearing and discuss why they have to dress this way.

There are many ways to make Moon feet:

- Tape bubble wrap around children's feet, making sure it's really thick underneath their soles. They'll love the popping noises as they walk.
- Cut out large footprints (at least twice the size of children's actual feet) from a thick corrugated cardboard box and attach them to the children's own shoes with string or tape.
- Put wellies on the wrong feet. Choose a pair of boots that are a few sizes bigger than the child's own feet for an added challenge.

Now walk like an astronaut around the familiar parts of the garden. Try to scale some steps, climb a couple of rungs of a climbing frame ladder, or run through the sandpit. Remember, children's bodies are changing and growing every day, so they are biologically programmed to adapt to these alterations in body volume and centre of gravity.

Clowning around

"Clowning is a comical and colourful imaginative play opportunity!"

Clowning, mime and ad lib performances have a rich and culturally diverse history. In many countries, exaggeratedly made up and extravagantly dressed actors were used to satirise establishment figures or as a way of attracting attention to protests.

Create a special clowning 'grab and go' box, complete with oversized garments, lengths of sparkly and shiny fabric (use pegs for draping), extra large shoes, wigs and odd props such as plastic flowers or windmills.

Simple clowning games work really well as warm-ups to a physical activity outdoors:

- **Pass it on:** One child in the circle makes a silly face or gesture and the child on their left must 'pass it on' to the child on *their* left and so on until it has gone all the way round the circle.
- **Let's all:** One child calls out, 'I know! Let's all . . .' and suggests an action, such as '. . . hop on one leg' or '. . . run around the tree'. The group replies, 'Yes! Let's all [do the action]!' and then carries out the instruction, moving across the whole space, before returning to hear the next child's instruction.
- **Equal and opposite:** Call out an action, for example, 'stand on your LEFT leg' or 'stand still!' After you've given a few instructions, tell children that they now need to do the *opposite* of your instruction, for example, stand on their RIGHT leg or run up and down on the spot.

Super noodles

"Pool noodles are open-ended, flexible, downright silly and great fun!"

Pool noodles — those long, brightly-coloured foam 'sausages' — are interesting resources and can support a variety of physical and imaginative play scenarios. Pipe lagging is similar, though usually slightly narrower in diameter and split along its length with a hollow centre.

Taking it further

Use a noodle to act out a motion and ask children to copy you, like in follow-the-leader. Think about developing hand-eye coordination skills, or upper body strength, so motions such as waving the noodle above your head, tossing it from one hand to the other and stepping over it are good motions to try.

Bonus idea ★

If you have pond dipping nets for use at your own setting or further afield, slide a short length of pipe lagging onto the handle and tape each end with waterproof duct tape. This will stop the net from sinking, should it be dropped in the pond!

To really make the most of pool noodles in the activities below you'll need an abundant supply. Cut a few of the noodles in half or into thirds to provide more manageable lengths for very young children.

- Gather a group of five or six children and give each one a noodle. Standing in a circle, each child should offer one end of their noodle to any other child to hold. Soon, you'll have a knot of noodles. The trick is to untangle the knot without letting go of the noodles. Children will need to establish who's holding which noodle and bend their bodies over and under the noodles in order to set themselves free.
- Teach children how to throw a noodle in a one-armed javelin style, and then set up hanging hoops or buckets for children to aim their noodles into. Chalk point scores onto the ground.
- Play hockey with young children. Use a soft foam ball and set up a special pitch so that children can practise hitting and stopping the ball without interfering with other children's play. Chalk goals onto the walls or ground to add an extra challenge.

Concentric chalk circles

"Our music specialist regularly uses the concentric circles to get children moving in opposite directions as they sing in parts."
Sue Humphries

Painted or chalked markings have always played an important role in children's play, from simple hopscotch through to complex painted games on playgrounds. A set of coloured concentric circles painted onto the playground can be a focal point for learning and play for generations of children.

Use chalk or playground marking paint to draw coloured concentric circles on the playground (see Taking it further below). Fill each band of the circle up with coloured chalk, if you can. Make the whole thing big enough to allow plenty of children to use it at the same time and try the following activities:

- Use the circles for warm up activities before a physical development session outdoors.
- Invent speed and agility games using the coloured bands as bases, for example, 'Three girls on the green! Four boys on the red! One girl on the white! Two boys on the orange!'
- Give children measuring resources such as rulers, measuring tape, trundle wheels, and metre rulers and encourage them to measure parts of the circle. Introduce terms such as *outline*, *half*, *whole* and even perhaps *radius* and *circumference*. Supply clipboards and pens to allow mark making and tally charts.
- Bring out string, ropes, hosepipes and concertina tubes – how many will it take to go around the whole of the circle?

Taking it further

Use a piece of chalk on the end of a long length of string, the other end of which is tied to a stick, to create perfect circles. The length of the string will be the radius of the circle. Each band of the concentric circle should be at least the width of an adult foot. Use an oil-based or specialist playground marking paint so that it is long-lasting. Start with the inner circle and wait until it's completely dry before painting the next one.

Mark making with a difference

"These are great ideas that will stimulate boys' enthusiasm for mark making."

Simple design changes and detailing, as well as appropriate resourcing can motivate reluctant writers to experiment with mark making. The key here is to move away from the formal indoor environment and embed mark making in self-initiated activities.

These activities will help to make mark making meaningful and relevant:

- A simple space divider provides definition between zones of different activities, but can also be designed to encourage writing tasks. In a role-play scenario, children may be more likely to pick up a pencil to write (for example, an 'MOT report' in a garage workshop set-up) if there is an elbow-height ledge to lean on rather than a table to sit down and write at. Reluctant writers will often mark make if the writing is an incidental activity associated with a role-play scenario that interests them. For imaginative play scenarios, boys enjoy being outdoors making MISSING posters for a lost animal, road signs for wheeled toys, or site instruction notices for a building site.
- Clipboards or chalkboards, stored outdoors where children can access them independently, can encourage the use of pencils and chalks as part of imaginative scenarios.
- Provide loose chalk and designate pavement art spots to encourage drawing and writing.
- If you have a mud kitchen, remember that mud can be a great writing medium, using sticks and branches as 'pencils' and 'brushes'.

By Felicity Robinson

Taking it further

Maps and charts can also be used to engage children to make marks for a purpose. A large chalkboard can be used to encourage map drawing. Make a start by attaching photos of familiar site features to the board, and encouraging children to draw the routes between them as a 'map' – then follow the same routes on the ground.

Bonus idea ★

Try mark making with wheeled toys by riding them though puddles and writing numbers or letters with the watery wheels! Add poster colour to the puddles to enhance the fun and creativity.

Journey sticks

"Even in our tiny garden, children find 'treasure' to record their journeys."

Journey sticks are an ancient concept that allows us to share and document our experiences of travelling. They are simple to create and work equally well in vast forests, on beaches, at the local park or in your own pre-school garden.

For this activity you will need a stick for each child and a bag full of elastic bands.

- Twist the elastic bands onto the stick at regular intervals, ensuring that each one is tight enough not to fall off, but loose enough to allow children to pull it. The length of the sticks and the number of elastic bands will depend upon the attention span and physical dexterity of the children as well as the journey location.
- Ask children to find interesting objects on their journey (for example, feathers, stones, twigs, scraps of paper or shells), and place them on the stick by trapping them under an elastic band, starting at one end and working their way towards the other so that there is some idea of chronology embedded into their journey evidence.
- At the end of their exploration, ask children to tell you: what they found, why they chose each object, where it was and what it means. The sticks make a fascinating and colourful display so find a piece of soft earth big enough to push them all into in order to show off the treasure.

Teaching tip

Make this activity trickier for older children by replacing the elastic bands with pre-cut lengths of string so that they have to practise knot tying on the journey. Longer sticks require more physical dexterity to handle and will take longer to fill.

Bonus idea ★

Use journey sticks to stimulate storytelling by pre-attaching objects to a stick and asking children to suggest what sort of journey you've been on and what you did on the journey based on the objects found on the stick.

Beanbag golf

"Children come back to beanbag golf time and again."

Create a gloriously simple game of golf using beanbags and the features of your garden. Target games like this are great for hand-eye coordination, and by adjusting the length of the 'fairway', this one works for children of any ability.

To get started, choose nine features around the garden to be your 'holes' — for example, a part of the sandpit, the climbing frame, a shed, a gate, etc. Each hole needs to be labelled clearly with its own number, from 1–9. In front of the first hole use chalk to draw a line (or use a length of string or rope) that is approximately three metres from the target.

- Children begin by standing on the chalk line and accurately aiming their beanbag at the first hole.
- If the child is able to hit the hole in the first throw, they gain one point. Each further throw to reach the hole adds another point.
- Children mark their score for each hole on a tally chart.
- Children aim for each subsequent hole by starting at the preceding one. The number of throws it takes to reach the next hole represents their score.
- The winner is the child with the fewest points — the one who took the least number of throws to reach the ninth hole.

Enabling environments

Part 3

Start as you mean to go on

"All beginnings are delightful, the threshold is the place to pause."
Johann Wolfgang von Goethe

The power of first impressions is strong. What does the entrance to your outdoor space say to children and parents about how you value outdoor play? The entrance and transition space are a vital element in the journey towards high-quality outdoor play. They help children establish their location, inspect the play potential and evaluate what they might do next.

Teaching tip

It's tempting to use your covered transition space as an extension of the classroom – but it should be so much more. Make the most of covered spaces by thinking about what they *add* to learning experiences and how they can make learning memorable – for example, by enabling more active storytelling, or hide and seek number recognition.

Taking it further

Work with a local artist to design and create beautiful new gates for your garden. Children will gain much from the memorable experience of collaborating with an artist and with one another. This unique artwork will also reflect your setting's ethos and show how you value your children and the community they live in.

Show that your outdoor space is a place of purposeful, exciting learning:

- Create a permanent noticeboard by the door, and change the displays regularly. For example, show recent photos of children playing; summarise the day's plan for outdoors; display outdoor-related requests and reminders for parents (such as, 'Wellies tomorrow, please!').
- Enable passers-by to glimpse activity. Children want to feel connected to their community and being able to watch the world go by is important to them. Don't be tempted to close off your entire garden; leave small gaps in the hedge or create peep holes in the fencing.
- Don't be obsessive about keeping the garden tidy – this is not Hampton Court Palace Flower Show! Allow children to occupy the space, but zone activity so that it doesn't become chaotic. See Idea 24, Zone in, for more details. Children need to know that they can leave a task and come back to it later, without finding it tidied away.
- Decorate trees and fences adjacent to entrances. Christmas baubles are fun all year round, as are strings of beads, shells and twigs on string and wind chimes.

Sun safe

"Slip on a shirt, slop on sunscrean, slap on a hat, seek shade, slide on sunnies – simple as that!" www.sunsmart.com.au

Australian families are very familiar with the phrase, 'Slip, slop, slap', but it is excellent advice for everyone! To make the most of the weather all year round, it's important to be prepared and to ensure children understand the health value of sunshine and know how to stay safe on sunny days (rare as they may be).

These activities will help you to plan ahead for sunny days:

- Make a double-sided weather sign with a sun on one side and an umbrella on the other. Explain to children that when they see the 'sun' side, it means wear a hat, cover their arms and try to play in the shade.
- Encourage dressing up! Keep a selection of floppy hats, long-sleeved shirts and crazy sunglasses in a box close to the doors to your garden/outdoor play area.
- Write to parents to inform them of your sun-safe policy – this could be part of your outdoor play policy (see Idea 3). Clarify when/how to apply sunscreen; ask parents to provide hats and sunscreen and remind them that limited exposure to sunlight (less than 15 minutes, usually) supplies children with vital Vitamin D.
- Keep a basket of sunscreens by the door to the garden.
- Ensure the den building box (see Idea 68, Dens and hidey-holes) is available every day so that children can create their own shady spots. Include a few umbrellas too, they are great fun to play with whatever the weather.

Teaching tip

Include 'Slip, slop, slap' in your Personal, Social and Emotional Development curriculum, encouraging children to take responsibility for self-care on sunny days. Share books about how other cultures deal with hot sun and invite children to talk to you about how they like to stay cool in the sun.

Taking it further

More information about sun safety, and how to use a sun-safe policy, can be found at www. sunsmart.org.uk

Curate a stick collection

"Our stick collection is the most enduring of all our resources!"

I make no apology for being a huge fan of this tactile, open-ended, free, naturally occurring and renewable resource. Children return to play with sticks time and time again, whatever the weather or the season. Curating a stick collection means you'll always have the right shape or size of stick for every play opportunity.

Teaching tip

Store sticks in a safe place – away from busy entrances or exits. Appropriately-sized sticks should be accessible to children, but be sure to show them how to transport sticks around the garden (for example, upright!). A bin is ideal for storing large sticks. Store the smaller ones that children can access every day in gardeners' flexible plastic trugs.

Taking it further

The stick book by Fiona Danks and Jo Schofield contains dozens of excellent stick games and craft ideas. Also, visit www.creativestarlearning.co.uk for practical examples of how to integrate sticks into the curriculum.

Whilst a few idiosyncratic sticks with crazy bark or twisting shapes are great fun to have, a collection of straight sticks is invaluable for digging, den building, beating out a rhythm, counting, mark making, journey sticks, artwork and more!

- Seek long, straight, narrow diameter sticks, and use sharp loppers to trim them to size. Trim off any side shoots or branches.
- Give children sanding blocks to smooth the cut ends. Sanding is a great physical activity in itself, requiring concentration and hand-eye coordination. Sanding blocks are cheap and much easier for small hands to use than sandpaper.
- Useful everyday stick lengths (10cm; 25cm; 50cm; 1m) are great for maths activities as well as free play. A few longer, heavier sticks (1.5m), with a bigger diameter are great for musical and rhythmic activities.

Sources of sticks include:

- Your garden and those of friends or family.
- The park or countryside, especially after a storm to collect larger sticks to trim to size.
- Local tree surgeons or landscape gardeners who can save long and straight sticks for you.

Making the most of the ground

"When you're that much nearer to it, the ground takes on a great deal more importance!"

If space is limited, it's important to make the most of every surface you have. The surface under your feet doesn't have to be boring Tarmac; make it work for your children by enriching their play. The hard surfaces in a play space are often maligned; in fact, they are far more flexible and versatile than you might imagine!

Leave at least one large area clear and free of markings so that children can create their own designs with chalk, water and mud.

A large circle made up of differently coloured concentric rings painted onto a hard surface provides a focus point for children − it can act as a circle time gathering point, a playground game 'base' and a stage for performances.

Instead of fixed play equipment, choose loose parts resources such as crates, hollow blocks and planks so that children can make their own challenging play structures. These can be stored away when not in use, allowing the space to be used in other ways.

Zoning an outdoor space can help manage the way it is used by 'space hungry' activities such as bikes and trikes. Use portable zoning resources such as planters on castors, logs and tree stumps so that the zones can be as large or as small as the activity and the number of children requires.

Use picnic blankets and cushions to create cosy seating areas whenever the weather or children's fancy allows.

Teaching tip

Think about storage outdoors − make sure the loose items you choose can be stored close to where they are likely to be used, otherwise you'll spend a great deal of time lugging things around.

Taking it further

If grass won't survive the hurly-burly of outdoor play at your setting, plant grass seed in tubs or in a large raised bed, so that children can still experience the coolness of grass on their cheek or the smell of freshly cut (with scissors!) grass.

Making the most of airspace

"Look up and think big."

In smaller settings, it's important to make the most of all the space you have, yet it's easy to forget to look upwards. This idea provides a collection of suggestions to help you think about stimulating your children's imaginations and encouraging physical development by exploiting what's above their heads.

Involving parents

A Hampshire setting invites its children to bring a windmill or wind spinner with them when they first join the setting. Parents are encouraged to find (or make) a windmill or spinner with their children, and bring it in on the first day, labelled with their child's name. All the windmills and spinners are attached to fences, walls or eaves around the play space. Multicoloured windmills and spinners of all shapes and sizes make an attractive and unusual display, which is updated each time a new child joins the setting.

- Provide beanbags, picnic blankets and cushions so children can lie down and cloud spot, plane spot or bird watch.
- Attach bird boxes high up in trees.
- Hang quoits or hula hoops from the outstretched branches of trees to create impromptu target practice games, or hang them quite close to the ground for children to clamber through as part of an obstacle course.
- Set up a rope pulley system from a window to a fence post or tree so that children can transport objects across the garden.
- Attach binoculars to an accessible high point, for example, at the top of a climbing structure, so that children can observe the land all around.
- Play with stomp rockets or make your own water rockets (see Idea 71, Rocket science).
- Make or buy periscopes to allow children to peer around corners and over fences.
- Screw stainless steel eyehooks into walls and fences, at least 2m above ground level – i.e. above adult head height. String, garden wire or wool looped randomly between the eyehooks creates a high-level web from which objects can be suspended – glinting CDs, fluttery ribbons, flapping flags, strings of beads or bottle tops, hula hoops, mirror letters, bird feeders . . . Move the features around every now and then and add new objects to maintain children's curiosity.

Making the most of outdoor walls and fences

"We have little more than an alley for outdoor play – making use of the walls, ground and air above us has helped to extend the outdoor play opportunities on our doorstep."

Play doesn't just happen at eye level. Use the vertical surfaces around you for storage, display, den building and so much more. Leave no space unused!

- Are awkward-shaped resources taking up too much room in the shed? If they're waterproof, store them on wall hooks or in wire baskets on the wall or fence outdoors – hula hoops, quoits, plastic balls, washing up bowls and wheelbarrows can all live against a wall.
- Attach two or three wire 'over bath' caddies to the wall to allow children of different heights to take part in weaving activities. You could also glue mesh into a timber frame, which you could hinge to the wall. This creates a weaving frame that will fold flat against the wall.
- Fix exterior mirrors to the walls to give the impression of a larger space than you actually have; mirrors behind planting beds work really well too. A convex security mirror is enormous fun, distorting children's bodies and their surroundings – install it at child height rather than on the roofline.
- Paint targets onto the wall and use small, soft balls to minimise the risk of children getting hurt by rebounds. Make the targets attractive to look at, and plan to repaint them every couple of years.

Teaching tip

When planning outdoor activities, consider the types of experience or developmental milestones you're aiming for. This will help you to identify appropriate activities and the resources you need. You'll also be able to justify any costs by explaining exactly how the children will benefit from the investment.

Mud kitchen

"Our messy kitchen menu includes garden soup, muddy potions, The three bears' porridge and more!"

Given the chance, most children will happily dig, mix and splosh in the soil outdoors! By planning for mud play, you can not only satisfy the desires of the most hands-on children, you can help the more reluctant explorers to investigate mud at their own pace, using familiar resources.

Involving parents

Parental support is vital for a successful mud kitchen. Invite parents to donate items from their own kitchens and to come along to observe the children at play. Ask parents to watch how children interact, how they communicate with one another, how they accurately handle equipment and how they take turns. These are all essential skills for young children, so allowing parents to observe how mud play supports these skills will help make the case for messy play.

Taking it further

For further suggestions about how to equip them and exploit their potential see the free, illustrated booklet, *Muddy Faces*, by Jan White www. muddyfaces.co.uk.

Here are some top tips for making your own messy mud kitchen.

- Allocate a space for mud play, for example, use a worn out patch of grass to create your mud kitchen.
- Create a boundary to prevent mud spreading all over and to contain the resources.
- Ensure there is a water supply nearby – a tap, a water butt or the end of a hose – and plenty of vessels for transporting water to the soil.
- Be generous with your resources – have not just one colander but five; not just one bowl but ten; have 20 wooden spoons, all different sizes.
- Choose robust objects that will stimulate the imagination and provide tactile stimulation too, for example, engraved goblets, stainless steel balti dishes and mosaic plant pots.
- Ensure children are appropriately clothed for mud play. Nothing will limit the life of a mud kitchen like a bunch of angry parents!
- Children should take responsibility for cleaning up the mud and themselves at the end of the session – provide child-sized mops and brooms and ensure they are able to change their footwear before going back indoors.

My thinking place

"Quiet thinking places were our response to children's need for silence and solitude."

Even in the busiest outdoor play spaces it is possible to create places (or enable periods of time) that foster peace and reflection. All children will benefit from the opportunity to spend time on their own simply observing and absorbing the natural world round them.

Inspect your outdoor space and using a sheet of A3 paper, sketch out a plan of the area, including fences and gates, trees and shrubs, play equipment, raised beds, the sandpit etc. Make multiple copies of the plan and ask colleagues to mark the really popular areas of your outdoor space. Do this on different days of the week and at different times of the day.

Compare all the maps. Are there any spaces that could be designated quiet thinking places? These don't have to be places that no child goes to, but instead places that are less well used, tucked away out of sight.

Designate these as quiet spaces. Consider what might need to be done to enable solitude, for example, using portable trellises or a sheet strung between fence posts or trees to provide privacy; planting a screen of bamboo or tall grasses.

Be careful to ensure that you don't inadvertently create isolated spaces; a thinking place can still be an observable place. Ideally, adults should be able to see over or into the space without having to approach it too closely.

Teaching tip

If you know a child would benefit from time in one of your thinking places, try to draw other children away from the area. This isn't always going to be possible, but consider attracting children to a part of the garden that is a distance away from the thinking place.

Bonus idea

Plan a silent walk around the outdoor space, dropping children off at their own quiet points. Take up to eight children with you, agreeing a hand signal in advance to indicate when a child should sit down. Give each child a square of carpet to sit on. Once all children have been sitting alone, for a few minutes, repeat the route, silently collecting each child as you go. Afterwards, ask what the experience of solitude felt like, remembering that some may not want to share their thoughts.

Zone in

"Zoning the area helped manage children's expectations and allowed every child to play unhindered by other activities."

Every child has the right to follow their interests and fascinations outdoors, from the children racing on their Formula 1 trikes to the child absorbed in examining a snail on a stone. Zoning allows all activities, big or small, communal or private, to coexist in even the smallest of spaces.

Draw or print off two or three copies of a plan of the whole of your outdoor space. You'll need felt tip markers, photographs of the space in use and a large sheet of paper.

Examine the photographs of the space and discuss what children are doing and what they are playing with. Does the time of day or the time of year make a difference to how the space is used? On the sheet of paper, write down all of the *types of activity* occurring outdoors, for example, 'growing veggies' or 'sand play'. Try to write these randomly on the sheet so that no single activity is more prominent than the others.

Ask what kind of space is needed for each of these activities? Using a different colour marker pen, annotate each activity with a type of space, for example, 'quiet' or 'sheltered'. Do any of the activities require specific features or facilities (for example, a tap)? Add these notes too.

On one of the plans, draw 'bubbles' to indicate roughly where each type of space is located – you may find there is more than one bubble for each type of space and that they overlap: the aim is not to divide the space but to share it. Include storage areas and routes through the space – for example, entrances and exits to the building and the site. These routes are key and shouldn't be blocked.

Examine how you could organise the space so that competing activities don't overlap, or are relocated to allow them to have their own space. Are there activities that could happily coexist if they were managed differently? For example, in some settings, bikes and trikes are only available for two days a week – on other days, the space is used for large-scale construction and dens.

Taking it further

Use the other plans of the space to try out different ways to more effectively share the space. Some ideas may require longer term changes, but others could be tried out over a few weeks to see if the changes have a positive effect on the quality of play.

Bonus idea

A playful but clever way of establishing children's preferred seating arrangements outdoors is to experiment with chairs from indoors. Bring lots of chairs into the play space, and leave them in a big group. Explain to the children that they can move the chairs anywhere and use them in any way they like. Observe where the chairs go, what they are used for and how children group them; you'll need to 'dynamically' risk assess this activity – in other words, use common sense in enabling children to take risks. Take plenty of photographs during play to illustrate children's ideas and preferences. You could also sketch chair locations onto your site plan. Carry out the chair activity over several days, enabling children to really think about their favourite spaces and explore how their preferences change depending on the weather, the time of day and the number of children outdoors at the time.

Bottle babies

"Quick! We are blasting off and we need rocket fuel! Get more bottle babies!"

Bottle babies are a free resource that feed the imagination and build core muscle strength. These water-filled, upcycled, two-litre bottles can be used as rocket fuel canisters, bricks for building, drinks for tea, and sometimes they can even be babies!

Parents and teachers are always looking for free, reusable, and open-ended resources that will serve multiple purposes. Children can use these two-litre bottles in a variety of imaginary ways. It is important to use two-litre bottles as these provide the right weight to size ratio to build core strength and coordination in young children. While they are building these important muscle sets by carrying these bottles around, they are negotiating how to carry this weight AND imagining a variety of uses!

It is very easy to make and use bottle babies:

- Collect lots of two-litre bottles. Ask parents to bring in empty bottles from home.
- Fill almost to the top with water.
- Optional: add paint, food colour, stones, sticks, beads, etc.
- Twist cap on firmly.
- Introduce the 'bottle baby' to the child.
- Alternatively, you could make the bottle baby with the children.
- The more bottle babies you have, the better.

By Lesley Romanoff

Naturally playful

Part 4

Pictures and potions

"Mark making is a basic, primeval urge. There's something joyful and wild about crushing and mixing natural ingredients."

Throughout history, humans have crushed berries, rocks, bark and other natural materials to make marks. The marking of walls and floors, faces, arms and bodies played an important role in the cultural development of the human race. Get your children mark making with natural ingredients.

The intense, vibrant colours of natural materials and different textures means making your own potions with them is great fun. There's lots of measuring and counting to be done too, and mixing potions demands physical dexterity and stamina.

- Collect your potion ingredients, for example, small pieces of bark, remains of burnt wood (i.e. charcoal), bright green leaves, chunks of natural chalk. You'll also need some water and each child will require a bowl for crushing and mixing, plus various cooking utensils including forks and wooden spoons. Make sure there are plenty of cloths, baby wipes or towels handy.
- Crush the ingredients in the bowl using hands or utensils. Add water to make runnier potions – you could thicken them up with cornflour or powdery chalk if necessary.
- Children will enjoy marking their arms and legs with the potions, or mark making on the ground. Natural chalk makes a fabulous gloopy mixture that lends itself to handprints on asphalt or lengths of coloured paper. Charcoal and water make an excellent black pigment.

Leafy letters

"If you could tell the forest how it makes you feel, what would you say?"

This delightful idea works well all year round and encourages children to think about and share adjectives and verbs to describe how being in the forest makes them feel. Leaves are nature's answer to sticky notes and they make a stunning and unusual display.

Take the group into a wooded area. This should be a space where you can immerse yourself in the trees and perhaps escape from everyday ambient noise.

Collect leaves from the ground – each child should collect three or four and place them in a pile. Spread out a little and ask everyone to be silent. Listen carefully to the sounds you can hear, for example, birdsong, swishing branches, crunching leaves, scurrying animals. Enjoy the atmosphere of the woodland. Try to sit or lie on the ground quietly for five minutes.

Ask, 'How does being in the forest make you feel?' Share the statement, 'In the woods I can be . . . ' and ask the group to describe their emotions. Using marker pens, write one word or phrase on each leaf.

If children suggest the same words, try to encourage them to think of synonyms, for example, for 'amazed' ask them to ponder other ways of expressing this emotion, such as 'shocked', 'surprised' or 'happy'.

Display the annotated leaves back indoors on a table, or place them all in a big bowl, with a sign above saying, 'In the woods, I can be . . . '

By Lily Horseman

Teaching tip

More able children will want to write on the leaves for themselves - take a few sheets of paper with you so that they can copy your spellings. For your less confident writers, allow them to make marks in any way that suits them.

Treasure baskets

"These baskets often spark mathematical thinking – patterns, shapes and counting are frequently the core activity."

Treasure baskets are now commonly used in early years to stimulate children's curiosity and imagination – but does your setting have them outdoors? Make the most of abundant natural materials all year round to offer your youngest children fascinating opportunities for exploration.

Teaching tip

Storing natural materials collections in beautiful containers is an important part of the attraction they hold for young children. Budget to replace the baskets themselves every couple of years as they begin to wear out or disintegrate. Charity shops and car boot sales are great places to look for baskets.

Heuristic play is using collections of everyday objects (most definitely *not* toys) to stimulate children's curiosity and imagination. Store your heuristic play items in attractive baskets and keep them outdoors in a place that children can easily access. Hang a dustpan and brush nearby so that older children can tidy up after they have finished and take responsibility for returning the objects to their treasure baskets at the end of a play session. Items for your treasure baskets:

- **Natural resources** – acorns, cob nuts (these are spiky), shells, wooden disks, pebbles, chunks of natural chalk, sycamore helicopters, conkers.
- **Wooden and plastic materials** – coloured bottle tops (washed), cardboard tubes, lollipop sticks, cotton reels, wooden beads, wooden spoons, dolly pegs, curtain rings, fabric, jam jar lids.
- **Shiny objects** – steel and aluminium kitchen utensils, dishes, spoons, silver emergency blankets, boules (these are heavy), candlesticks, plastic mirrors, milk bottle tops (washed).

The additional space, the sun and shadows, breezes and noise will all have an effect on what children choose to do with the objects. Use your observations to support children's continuing progression, for example, making the most of their interest in laying trails or constructing small world villages.

Crowning glory

"Making crowns marks the start of our super spring celebrations!"

In spring, the abundance of fresh green leaves, vibrant flowers and intense smells is beguiling. Spring crowns are made by weaving flowers, leaves and small twigs through a hat made from cardboard and florists' wire. The finished effect is like having a flowering nest on your head!

Cut corrugated cardboard strips approximately 5cm deep and long enough to wrap around a child's head. Make plenty of randomly placed holes in each one using a hole punch. These will allow children to weave their natural materials in and out of the cardboard, using the florists' wire to hold them in place. Write each child's name on the inside of their crown and then glue or staple both ends of the cardboard.

Collect natural materials to decorate the crowns with, for example, blossom, berries or flowers. Soft-stemmed shrubs such as ivy and clematis are ideal for poking through the punched holes but be sure to remind children not to taste any of the materials. Give children short lengths of florists' green taped wire to help them place the sprigs exactly where they want them.

This task requires concentration and care. Weaving in and out of the punched holes can be tricky, and younger children may need the holes enlarged. Once the crowns are made, plan a parade around the garden, pointing out the signs of spring and stopping to talk about how living things change over the seasons.

Teaching tip

Younger children will need help with this activity as the weaving and poking can be fiddly. Shorter sprigs of greenery and staples can help speed up the process. Also, children could glue petals and leaves onto their crowns rather than weaving them.

Bonus idea

Make Green Man faces by gluing leaves all over a cardboard mask to create a 'camouflaged' face. Use elastic to hold the mask in place. See Idea 33 for more about Green Man masks.

Feed the birds

"This is a messy idea – so the children enjoyed it even more!"

Birds are beautiful and fascinating creatures. Observing them, sketching them and caring for them help children to begin to explore the natural world and their own responsibilities within it. Making the bird feeders can be quite fiddly so care will be needed, but the activity will develop hand-eye co-ordination as well as providing excellent opportunities for language and storytelling.

Taking it further

Upturned yoghurt pots are also great moulds for lard bird feeders, as are hollowed out halves of grapefruit, plastic drinking bottles, aluminium cans, small terracotta plant pots and even old teacups.

Bonus idea ★

To make the feeders with lard, allow the lard to reach room temperature and cut it into cubes. In a large bowl, squash the lard and birdseed together until it makes a thick, sticky mixture. Press it into the cookie cutters and poke a short length of a drinking straw into the mixture and put in the fridge for an hour or so to set. Loop a length of string through the hole made by the straw and hang outdoors!

You will need: a large bag of fine birdseed, hot water in a large bowl, gelatine sachets (a 12g sachet will usually make approx. ½ litre of gelatine), a whisk, an assortment of cookie cutters, lengths of twine/wool, greaseproof paper.

- Mix half a litre of very hot water with four sachets of gelatine and whisk until dissolved.
- Add birdseed to the bowl a handful at a time and mix carefully until all of the gelatine water has been absorbed.
- Whilst the mixture cools, lay the cookie cutters onto the greaseproof paper, and cut lengths of twine or wool to around 30cm.
- Half fill each cookie cutter with the birdseed mixture and press down gently.
- Place one of the doubled over lengths of twine into the cookie cutter (looped end in the mixture) and then fill up the remaining space with more mixture. Press it down gently.
- Leave the shapes to harden overnight – turn them over on the greaseproof paper before you leave for the day.
- Release the shapes from the cookie cutters and hang outdoors!

Scavenger hunt

"I always need ideas for rainy day scavenger hunts – for parents and tots!"

A twist on the traditional scavenger hunt, these clues will help children get outdoors on a rainy day and explore a shiny, noisy, slippery new world. Forest School practitioners are used to making the most of their beautiful environments, whatever the weather, and many of these suggestions are tried and tested by them.

For this hunt, consider asking children (assisted by their parents) to photograph objects rather than collecting them. This means everyone can 'collect' very delicate items or objects that they might not actually be able to reach – and then leave them for others to enjoy. Ask them to find the following:

- Something that will collect raindrops
- Something a bug could shelter in
- Something that absorbs water/repels it
- Something shaped like a raindrop
- Something with one of the colours of the rainbow in or on it (i.e. ROYGBIV)
- A cobweb hung with water drops or a puddle reflecting a tree
- Something with a 'wet' smell
- Something with a different texture when it's wet
- Something that doesn't belong
- Using 'exploring sticks', the deepest puddle and the squelchiest mud
- Something that floats
- Something that sinks
- Something that is dry on a wet day
- The driest place in the garden.

Teaching tip

You don't really need any equipment for a scavenger hunt, but you could lay out a tarpaulin on the ground to display the 'found' treasures. Litter pickers will allow your smaller children to reach inaccessible objects and treasure bags or baskets are always fun to use.

Taking it further

Use this activity to develop mathematical thinking. Give children clipboards, sheets of laminated paper and whiteboard markers to create tally charts and encourage them to think about lengths, shapes and weights of found objects by laying them out in order. Collect one of an object, two of another, three of another and so on, choosing higher numbers suitable for each child's understanding of numbers.

Hapa Zome

"This fantastic activity makes the most of boisterous children's energy to create something beautiful."

Hapa Zome is a Japanese art form that creates stunning prints by pounding the pigment out of leaves and flowers into a piece of cloth. This type of printing has been around for centuries, but textile artist and 'botanical alchemist', India Flint, has taken it in new directions, and it's now a common activity used in Forest School environments.

Teaching tip

The plant dyes can be washed but won't last forever. Help them last longer by steam ironing the fabric once the dye is dry, or use a fixative bath – boil the fabric in three parts water to one part vinegar for an hour, then rinse clean.

Taking it further

Read more about *Hapa Zome* printing at www. kindlingplayandtraining. blogspot.co.uk and at India Flint's website www. indiaflint.com

For each child you will need a length of pale cotton fabric and a hammer.

- Collect flowers, leaves and grasses. Plants with plenty of moisture in them create the most vibrant prints; wax-coated or dry plants are less effective. Try dandelions, bluebells, pansies, buddleia and thick, veiny leaves. Avoid berries as they squash and spread rather than simply transferring their colour. Place the piece of cotton onto a flat surface and arrange the flowers and leaves on top, using just one half of the cloth. Fold the cloth over so that the flowers and leaves are completely covered.
- Bash the flowers and leaves hard. A hammer is perfect for this job, but a smooth, hand-sized pebble or even the end of a thick stick will work. Keep bashing – it takes a few minutes to really draw out the pigments. Children should take care to bash all around the edge of the flowers and leaves in order to create an accurate image of the plant material.
- Unfold the cloth and compost the bashed plant material. What's left will be a wonderful print of the plant.

Green Man clay faces

"The two Green Man faces by the doors of our local church fascinated children, so we decided to make our own using leaves and tiny cones we found in our garden."

Clay is a wonderful resource, sorely underused outdoors. Its slippery, tactile qualities lend themselves to messy play outdoors and these 'secret' clay faces will surprise and delight until nature takes its course and they dry out and crumble back to dust. Adapt the Green Man myth to suit the age of the children, focusing on the rebirth and springtime elements.

- Show the children photographs of carved Green Man faces and describe where they can be found – there is lots of information about the Green Man myth online.
- Collect a big pile of natural materials, particularly leaves of different sizes, textures and shapes. You could also collect nuts, seeds or flowers, depending on the time of year. Small conkers and cones make attractive additions to Green Man faces.
- Children should choose a semi-hidden location for their face, and then press a handful of clay onto the surface of their location (for example, a tree trunk, fence panel, piece of play equipment, shed). A roughly textured surface such as timber will help the clay adhere for longer.
- Mould the clay into a face – making indentations for the eye sockets, a shaped nose, lips and a chin. Take care to make sure it remains stuck to its location.
- Use the natural materials collection to decorate the clay faces. The aim is to cover as much of the clay with leaves and greenery as possible, using other items such as the petals or cones to highlight features.
- Take a tour of your Green Man faces.

Teaching tip

Carry out this activity with small groups at a time. That way, the location of each Green Man face stays secret until other children go looking for them, or happen upon them by chance.

Bonus idea ★

Where does clay come from? Find a place in the grounds where it's okay to dig a deep hole – and dig! Dig as deeply as you can, taking soil samples every 10cm or so and keeping them in jam jars to allow children to compare the samples. You may find your own clay supply, or flints, chalk, slate or even a fossil or two!

Tree dressing

"We celebrate our trees all year round."

Tree dressing is an ancient tradition and takes place in communities all around the world for diverse reasons and at different times of the year, but you can celebrate trees every day.

Teaching tip

Remember to risk assess this activity – if you plan to hang objects high up the tree then observe ladder safety guidance.

Taking it further

Learn more about tree dressing traditions around the world, plus other events that celebrate local distinctiveness in the UK, such as Apple Day, by visiting the Common Ground website: www.commonground.org.uk.

Bonus idea ★

Once the tree is dressed, use it as a focal point in the setting – visit it to talk about the tree and its decorations, for stories under its shady boughs or to make up poems and tall tales inspired by the mysterious objects hanging in the tree.

The most obvious way to dress a tree is adorn one with Christmas decorations. This is a good way to introduce the concept to children.

- Take a tour of the garden with the children; what words can they use to describe their trees? Think about mathematical language (biggest, tallest, widest, next to) as well as lyrical, descriptive words (beautiful, bursting, swishy). How long have the trees been here? How can we tell? What kind of trees are they?
- Choose particular times of year to celebrate trees – for example, Diwali, the first day of spring or National Tree Week. You could organise your own personalised celebration (perhaps in memory of someone important to the setting), inviting parents and the local community into your setting to help with the decorating, or maybe adopt a tree in a local park or street.
- In autumn, collect fallen leaves, laminate them and reattach them to bare branches in winter.
- Decorate your tree with beads, baubles, wind chimes, bunting, laminated drawings and paintings, bric-a-brac, flags or natural objects (for example, conkers in a willow tree, corks, shells).

Grow your own, pick your own, cook your own!

"When he finally ate it, it was the first carrot he'd ever agreed to try!"

Healthy eating is a vital part of the health messages settings promote to children and families. Persuading children to eat vegetables can be tricky so growing, picking and eating your own produce is one way of convincing children to try something new.

Vegetables can be grown in anything from an old wellington boot to a couple of tyres on top of one another or put a growbag or a couple of plastic troughs in a spare sunny corner.

Choose vegetable and fruit crops that grow relatively quickly and will be harvested when the setting is in session (i.e. not the summer holidays, if you're closed). Your local garden centre will be very happy to offer advice about timing, climate and crop yields for the seeds they sell. Crops such as cherry tomatoes, carrots, peas, courgettes, strawberries and pumpkins are all rewarding crops to grow, providing flowers, interesting foliage and plenty of butterflies and caterpillars. Choose a few species that can be eaten raw, so that children can taste the difference. Peas, in particular, are much sweeter when newly harvested and eaten raw.

Start the seeds off indoors on a sunny windowsill and take photographs to document progress. Children should make illustrated labels for each crop, including the date it was planted.

Taking it further

Use the growing period to introduce mathematical and problem solving queries: what recipes shall we try once we have our pumpkins? How tall will this runner bean plant get? How many more weeks until we can harvest the carrots? How many strawberries have turned red today?

Bonus idea ★

If you have the space, create a raised allotment bed. Raised beds make planting and caring for vegetables much easier and offer the opportunity to grow crops (or flowers) all year round.

Wormy world

"I think worms have five hearts because they *really* love the earth!"

Worms play a vital part in our own lives, decomposing waste, aerating and enriching soil and controlling pests. This idea shows you how a wormery can build children's confidence in and respect for the power of the natural world.

Teaching tip

Only use raw food scraps in the wormery and chop them into small pieces. Cooked food can attract vermin and large chunks are hard for tiny worms to digest!

Bonus idea ★

Fill a fish tank with garden soil (not potting compost) and find (or buy) lots of worms to go in it. Children will be able to observe the worms moving through the soil to collect the scraps, which they will then drag back down into the soil. Do the worms prefer particular types of waste? Which scraps disappear quickest? Why do the worms leave some of the scraps?

A wormery will allow children to observe worms in action close up. Wormeries (and worms) can be purchased from larger garden centres and online stores.

Although not cheap, a three-layered wormery demonstrates the process clearly and cleanly. Chopped up fresh waste is added to the top layer, the middle layer contains compost that worms are working on and the bottom layer holds compost that's ready to use on the garden. Worms move through the perforated plastic layers and will complete their life cycle within the wormery.

Worms can also be incorporated into a standard compost heap or bin, and will speed up the composting process. Regularly turn the compost so that children can observe the worms at work.

If you can't make or buy a wormery, bury chopped up kitchen waste such as carrot tops, potato peelings and broccoli stems, then dig it back up again a week later to see how it has decomposed. You should be able to see worms busy with the waste! Cover it back over with soil and leave for another couple of weeks before repeating the exercise and discussing what children notice about the waste scraps.

Inspiring outdoors

Part 5

Jurassic tyre

"We took small world play outdoors so it could be messier and noisier!"

Tyres are a tremendous 'free and found' resource and are a familiar sight in early childhood settings. Encourage children's imaginative play and communication skills by creating a prehistoric landscape for small world play.

Tyres should be thoroughly cleaned with a pressure hose before use. Make sure there are no worn patches on the rubber surfaces as the reinforcing wire inside the tyre could work free.

Try to secure a really huge tyre for this play scene, as it will be popular. Line the tyre with thick plastic and fill it with compost or soil to approximately 10cm below the top. As a tyre filled with soil is heavy and awkward to move, make sure it's in the right location before beginning the build!

Create a prehistoric landscape for small world dinosaurs to live in:

- Make mountains and rocky wastelands by placing rocks, pebbles and patches of gravel in the soil.
- Make a lake using a plastic or foil food container inserted into the soil and filled with water.
- Use clippings from shrubs and bushes to make temporary forests.
- Handfuls of woodchip and sand will create variations in surface texture for young children to experiment with.
- Make a cave with air-drying clay – children should use natural materials to camouflage the cave.

Bonus idea ★

Make tall planters by stacking the tyres. Painting them in colours that complement your outdoor features will help make tyres look more attractive, as will planting climbers or plants that will hang over the side (for example, strawberries). They can also be located across open spaces to delineate or 'zone' different areas of activity.

Micro-sketching

"Mini-viewers helped children to understand the meaning of a 'bug's-eye view'."

Help children to focus on the detail all around them. If we only take the time to look properly, we can find intricate and extravagant worlds in tiny snapshots. This activity uses cut-out shapes as viewfinders to help children sharpen their descriptive and observation skills.

Use a craft knife to cut a shape (your 'viewfinder') into the centre of pieces of A5 or A6 thin cardboard. Squares, circles and rectangles are simple for younger children to handle. Complicated shapes, such as stars, or abstract, random cut-outs will provide extra challenge for older or more able artists. Cut one shape in each piece of card and aim to have a viewfinder around 5–8cm across.

Provide children with mark making materials and clipboards and ask them to find something tiny to draw – it could be natural or man-made. They should place the viewfinder over the top of the object and examine it through the cut-out hole. Ask the children to describe what they detect through the viewfinder, before attempting to draw as much of the detail as they can. Hand held magnifying glasses and sharp pencils will help the children recreate small details.

Some children will find the sketching tricky, in which case encourage them to use descriptive and comparative language to express what they can see.

Teaching tip

For longevity, laminate each viewfinder, remembering to ensure there is a wide border around each piece of cardboard *and* the cut-out shape itself, so that dampness can't leak in. Cutting out the viewfinder shape allows the object to be viewed without being squashed.

Bonus idea

Take sketching to a macro scale by providing children with A3 sized clipboards, A3 paper and pastels (soft chalks) to draw a bigger vista. If possible, place children higher up than their usual line of sight, for example, on a table, on top of a climbing frame, or wedged (safely) in a tree.

Giant grass art

"In our 'instant win' society, it's good for children to understand that sometimes projects take a while to reach fruition – waiting for our grass pictures to 'develop' is a perfect example."

Grass needs light and water to grow; its green colour is the result of light reacting with chlorophyll to produce food for the grass. When light is withheld, chlorophyll won't photosynthesise so plants lose their green colour and turn yellow. This activity shows you how to use this natural phenomenon to create grass pictures that will develop and then fade away.

Teaching tip

It is good to carry out this idea over a holiday period, setting up the picture a week or so before the holidays and uncovering it on your return. The longer the grass is left covered, the greater the effect – and the longer it will take for it to turn green again.

This looks best when carried out on a large scale. The design could incorporate abstract patterns, or children could draw a picture or symbol – but keep it simple first time you try this! To cover the grass use:

- Heavy-duty black bin liners. Weigh them down, close to the edges, with stones, bricks or pieces of timber so that the bin liners don't blow away.
- Black tarpaulin, cut up. Remember as you cut it up that it works a little like a photographic negative – the pieces you cut out will receive light and stay green, the covered grass will go yellow.
- Found objects. Interesting patterns can be created with tyres, crates, lengths of timber, pebbles, etc. The objects should be heavy enough not to blow away.

Leave the grass covered for at least two or three weeks. For sneak previews, take a camera and ask the children to lift a corner of the bin liner or tarpaulin to see how the picture is 'developing'. When all of the grass has gone yellow, carry out a grand unveiling.

Cloud spotting

"Children love to watch clouds sail by, imagining stories and scenarios."

In the midst of their busy, chaotic lives, finding time out to daydream is an important aspect of a child's life. Build in some 'down time' for children and spend it gazing at the clouds and sharing your observations.

Cloud spotting is a restful, calming activity. Taking time out to lie on a blanket and ponder the sky compels us to be reflective and can be a useful tool to slow the pace of the day or to help children recalibrate their emotions.

Choose a day with plenty of scudding clouds – huge fluffy cumulonimbus clouds, or streaky cirrus are great for cloud spotting. Find a sheltered and (if possible) quiet place in the garden and lay out a couple of picnic blankets. Be sure to remind children not to look directly at the sun (ideally, lie facing away from the sun).

Cloud spotting is often compared to the Rorschach test – the symmetrical ink blots used in psychological tests. What can children see in the clouds? Do they all see the same thing? What happens when the cloud moves across the sky – do new shapes form? Children may not want to share their thoughts – quiet time is precious time, so don't insist on them describing what they see if they'd rather just contemplate the sky.

Teaching tip

Learn the names of a few of the basic and common cloud formations, so that you can tell children what they are.

Taking it further

The Cloud Appreciation Society has a website and an app that will help you identify other types of cloud formation (www. cloudappreciationsociety. org.uk). The app allows you to upload your own cloud pictures and includes other cloud spotters' images, some of which will make children laugh out loud.

Soundscape mind maps

"Quiet contemplation and huge clipboards encouraged our reluctant mark makers to slow down the pace and make up their own shapes and symbols."

Urban-dwelling children learn to tune out ambient noise; country dwellers become immune to the birdsong or farm machinery. Sometimes, it's worth tuning back into environmental sounds in order to truly appreciate the soundscape we live in. Making mind maps brings a tight focus to children's sense of hearing and encourages them to use their imagination to invent symbols to represent the sounds they hear all around them.

Teaching tip

Talk to children about tone, pace and pitch. Compare the sound of different birds, or car engines or trees rustling. Do all door slams sound the same? How would children represent that sound in symbols?

Taking it further

Use percussion instruments to represent the sounds you heard. Children could recreate these sounds from memory or by reviewing their mind maps and deciding what each symbol would sound like using an instrument. If all these sounds are played together, does the result sound similar to the original soundscape you listened to?

The key to this activity is to spend at least five minutes in total silence, just listening to the ambient sounds. Ideally, give each child their own personal space in which to sit and contemplate, before they choose mark making equipment. Listening in silence takes patience and commitment, and you will know which children are ready to tackle this task.

A3 sized clipboards are a simple but versatile resource and allow children to be more expansive and free in their mark making. Smaller A5 clipboards can encourage children to be very precise and delicate. Some children may prefer to make their marks with chalk on the ground. Providing a set of different mark makers will help children articulate their thoughts – for example, a set of black mark makers including charcoal, fine liners, marker pens, biros and soft and hard pencils gives children choice about the best way to represent sounds.

Children might create symbols such as twirls, dots, jagged lines, circles, cloud shapes, waves and squiggles. When they have finished, look at the mind maps together. Did children choose similar symbols to represent the same sounds? What inspired them?

Bags of dance

"It's razzle-dazzle time! Reuse unwanted charity bags to create dance resources that withstand the weather!"

Many households have lots of unused plastic charity bags, waiting to be re-purposed into simple dance resources such as shakers and ribbon sticks. No more hours wasted trying to wash commercially-available versions of these items or unpick the knots in the ribbons. Make, shake and enjoy!

To make these dance resources, ask children to find a stick roughly the same length as the distance between their elbow and fingertips and about the thickness of their thumb.

Ribbon sticks:

- Cut open the plastic charity bag so that you create the longest length of ribbon possible.
- Attach the ribbon to each stick with parcel tape.
- Enjoy playing with the ribbon – try, name writing, moving to music and casting spells.
- Get children to compare and swap sticks with friends, and try creating double or triple ribbon sticks.

Cheerleader shaker sticks:

- Cut open the plastic charity bag along its width, and cut strips approximately 25cm wide.
- To create the tassels, cut widthways into the plastic strip every centimetre or two, almost but not quite through to the other edge. Leave an uncut edge of plastic. It will look like a very long fringe.
- Put double-sided sticky tape along the uncut edge of the fringe, and wrap this around a stick a few centimetres from one end. Seal the double-sided sticky tape end of the fringe with parcel tape for extra security.
- Shake it, wave it, dip it in paint and create pictures with it!

By Juliet Robertson

Teaching tip

Practise scissor skills by cutting up charity bags and using the bits and pieces created to produce artwork, for example, fence weaving.

Taking it further

Use charity bags to create simple handheld kites to enable children to dance with the wind.

Music and movement

"Dancing in the garden, children can do their own thing without poking one another's eyes out!"

Dance is a joyful physical activity and one that benefits from mass participation – so it requires plenty of room to move. Where better to take dance and movement than outdoors into the play space? Outdoors, children's creative expression might be inspired by the natural world, or by the man-made environmental sounds, smells and sights.

Teaching tip

If you don't already have an external electrical socket at your setting, invest in installing a high quality, double external socket. It's much safer than using extension cables from indoors and along with an external tap and hosepipe, will be one of the best play value resources you'll ever pay for.

Bonus idea ★

Why not create a dance or street theatre performance or an exercise routine and take it out into your local community? Try a market square, shopping centre or park and see if you can attract passers-by to join in too – remember you may need permission from the landowner (and the children's parents) before you do this!

A robust CD or MP3 player, suitable for outdoor use is an early years setting is essential. Choose a model that will enable children to change the music themselves and, if possible, allow it and some of its CDs to live with other outdoor resources so that children don't have to choose between music indoors or out.

Curate a dance resource box, bursting with beautiful shimmery fabrics, ribbons on sticks, musical shakers and wrist or ankle bells. Extend or focus children's dance ideas by occasionally adding new objects such as masks, strips of fake fur, face paint tubs, silk flowers, a selection of large shells or even a favourite picture book.

A dedicated space for dance is valuable, allowing small groups of children to enjoy inventing their own routines; try to locate this away from other competing activities such as fast moving trikes or noisy climbing frames. Use the whole of your outdoor space when working with an entire cohort of children – mass participation in dance is uplifting and exhilarating and you can encourage children to make the most of the 'obstacles' in their way.

What can we hear?

"Our problem is that sound is not important in our culture. We know the world from the visual, not from the other senses. I had to be taught other ways of understanding." Bernie Krause, sound recordist, Wild Sanctuary

Sounds are all around us but often not listened to. Whether you're in an urban environment with cars rushing by or in a rural setting with just the sound of birds and the wind around you, these sounds all have an impact on our time outside. In this activity, children take time to sit quietly and discover more about what they can hear.

Encourage children to listen to the sounds around them when they are outside – birds singing in the trees, people walking by or the noise of traffic. This activity works best with a group of four–six children.

- Find a comfortable place to sit outside, with as few distractions nearby as possible.
- Ask the children to be as quiet as they can. You could also offer blindfolds to reduce visual distractions and heighten the other senses.
- Concentrate on the sounds all around. After a few moments of silence, ask a child to share what they can hear. Can others hear it too?
- First, ask the child to describe the sound – is it low or high, quiet or loud, sharp or soft, gravelly or smooth? You may want to offer up a choice between contrasting descriptive words the first time you try this out.
- When the child has described the sound, ask the group if they can identify it too.
- Repeat with the other children in the group.

By Mary Jackson

Teaching tip

Sometimes we think about the outdoors as a place in which to make noise, but learning how to sit quietly for a while is an important skill and one that children will need to develop. Children may experience noisy and hectic home lives so may not be used to sitting quietly. Start this activity with a small group of children, and build up the time for sitting quietly gradually.

Involving parents

Invite parents into your setting to sit quietly and listen with their children. Ask them to repeat the exercise at home, when they go on a walk or visit new places where the sounds around them might contrast with the familiar sounds of home and setting.

Sounds and symbols

"This activity allows us to include all children, regardless of their speaking ability."

How can you help children describe the sounds they hear when their vocabulary is limited? In this activity (which follows on well from Idea 44, What can we hear?) children use visual cues to express and represent different sounds and create unique artworks at the same time.

Teaching tip

Allow children to create unique symbols themselves rather than trying to influence the symbols they already know. It is likely that children will also interpret the sounds using their bodies (for example, jumping up and down to a marching sound) – ask them to think about what that movement would look like marked onto paper.

Taking it further

Give each child their own long piece of paper and ask them to create their symbols without letting anyone else see what they've done. Once all of the contrasting sounds have been played, compare the drawings children have made. Can they match up one another's symbols with the sounds they heard? Did everyone create the same sorts of symbols or are they all very different?

- Large sheets of paper, such as wall lining paper, are great for this. Lay these out in a place where you have plenty of room to move around the roll of paper, for example, on the ground or attached to a fence. Select some contrasting sounds, for example, you could play excerpts from a CD, listen to the sounds all around you, make a noise on a feature in the garden, or play sounds on an instrument. Think about contrasts such as loud and quiet, meandering and repeating, rhythmic and *avant garde*. Children don't need to know these words – they are just listening to what they can hear and interpreting it visually.
- Ask the children to think what these sounds might 'look like' if they were to draw them. If the sound is short and quick, it might look like a dot. Provide a variety of mark making items such as felt tips, crayons, pastels, chalk, finger paints, wet clay.
- The children then design an image of the sound they have described on a section of the paper roll.

By Mary Jackson

Making our own music

"Music is an outburst of the soul." Frederick Delius

You don't need musical instruments to make music. This activity helps children discover that music is all around them outdoors. Your outdoor setting offers opportunities for large scale, physically demanding percussion. Children will adore exploring their surroundings to find what sounds they can make by scraping, banging, twanging or blowing into objects they usually play on or with!

Children love being given permission to hit things, so find a place they can do this without harming anything (or anyone) and be clear that bashing the features and fixtures of the garden is not something they would normally do.

- Outdoors, ask the children to discover the sounds made by different surfaces when they walk, jump or run on them – is there a difference between grass and gravel, a drain cover and snow?
- Collect a selection of beaters, for example, wooden or metal spoons, small plastic bottles with lids on, whisks, small brushes. Take a walk around your outside space, testing out the different surfaces to see what sounds they make when hit with one of the beaters. Remember to think about vertical surfaces too (walls, fences, railings) and test whether the sound is different if the object is hit quickly or slowly.
- Try out different beaters on each surface to hear the alternative sounds they make. How noisy or quiet can they be? Do different parts of the feature make other sounds?

By Mary Jackson

Teaching tip

Ensure children get to use a variety of beaters and encourage them to use their whole bodies to make noises as well as being very precise and delicate. Show them a clip of percussionist Dame Evelyn Glennie, who is deaf, to see how she uses her whole body to help make the music.

Taking it further

Combine this activity with Idea 45, Sounds and symbols. Children should make their sounds and then create symbols to represent them. Once there is 'notation' for the sounds, children could 'perform' their musical sounds by demonstrating the sounds of the symbols you have created.

An artist's palette

"Pure drawing is an abstraction. Drawing and colour are not distinct; everything in nature is coloured." Paul Cezanne

Even in the most undeveloped outdoor space the range of colours, hues and shades is immense. Encourage children to examine subtleties of colour in more detail with these colour spotting ideas. Back inside their collections will inspire their own artistic masterpieces!

Involving parents

Ask parents to take their child to a DIY store to collect paint sample cards. These are great for colour matching, as each card has different shades of the same colour. Can children and their parents find exact matches outdoors in their own garden or at the park?

On stiff white A4 card, draw and cut out 'artist's palette' shapes. Cut a hole in the curved part of the palette where the artist's thumb would fit and stick short lengths of double-sided sticky tape around the palette; between 2cm and 4cm long is ideal.

Ask children to find natural examples of a particular colour – or range of colours – outdoors and to stick them onto the double-sided tape. You could mark each piece of tape with the initial letter of each rainbow colour (i.e. ROYGBIV) and ask children to find examples of those. Subtle but varying shades of one colour, (for example, green or grey) offer more challenge, especially if children attempt to arrange them on the palette from lightest to darkest.

Show children copies of paintings by the Impressionists and Pointillists, indicating how the artists vary shades of the same colour. Do any of the colours in the paintings match the colours on the children's palettes?

Ask the children to make their own Impressionist paintings using the artist's palettes and the colours they found outdoors.

Picture this

"The pictures children make in their minds are so much more memorable."

Help children view the familiar with fresh eyes by introducing extraordinary 'frames' to process what they see. From tiny cut-out viewfinders to repurposed junk, seeing the world from a different perspective promotes communication and language skills, as well as offering artistic opportunities.

These suggestions lead neatly into mark making work, but they are equally valuable as strategies to encourage children to talk about what they see, or create imaginative play scenarios.

- Make viewfinders by cutting out different shapes in the middle of A5 sheets. Make some of the cut-outs really tiny and others abstract shapes. Encourage children to look at objects through the viewfinders – for example, blades of grass, bricks or sand.
- Hold plastic clipboards (readily available online) against an object and ask children to replicate what they see by drawing directly onto the clipboard using dry wipe markers. When they hold the clipboard against a light coloured background, they'll see a 'skeleton' image of their object. Can other children guess what the original object was?
- Visit your local charity shops and car boot sales to scavenge old picture frames. Remove the pictures, the mounts (save these, for use with children's own artwork) the glass and the backing and detach any loose fixings from the frame. Use the frames for chalking 'framed' pictures onto the ground, touring the garden enclosing views of favourite places, 'photographing' each other or assembling artworks from found objects.

Teaching tip

Frames can also offer peaceful, thought-provoking solitary moments. Encourage children to take their chosen frame (viewfinder, clipboard or real frame) to a quiet spot and contemplate the view through it. There's no need to report back or draw or write; sometimes silent, contemplative time is sufficient to recharge emotional batteries.

Outdoor gallery

"Children should be able to see evidence of their learning all around them."

Think about the rooms you use every day. Are you documenting your children's progress so that they and their parents can see it? Are you going out of your way to use interior walls, windows, nooks and ceilings as an attractive, colourful and informative display of children's learning? What about outdoors?

Every setting understands the value of showing off children's work and it is very unusual to visit a setting whose walls are not filled with fabulous photos, paintings, alphabets and practitioner commentary. This documentation benefits everyone – children, who love seeing their work and themselves in photographs and enjoy recalling the stories behind the pictures; parents, who feel more connected with their child's life at the setting if they can see what they've been up to; and practitioners, who are able to reflect on their own practice and learn from their colleagues' by examining displays.

In order to raise the profile of the importance of outdoor play in the early years, it is vital that this good practice is continued outdoors, and that displays outdoors reflect the learning through play that is taking place. Use the same principles you use indoors – theme displays, change them regularly, involve children in their creation, blend text for children with text for adults, etc.

Make the most of the unique display features outdoors:

- Attach photographs and children's drawings to fences and gates with small cable ties, which are more secure and less fiddly than string or treasury tags. Use Blu-Tak™ to attach items to masonry.

- Dangle images and artefacts from trees, canopies and pergolas. Hang them no lower than children's eye level, to avoid entanglements.
- Tie words and phonic graphemes to places that will help children interpret them – for example, 'ee' on a tree trunk; 'wall' on the side of the building; or 'down' and an arrow at the top of the slide.
- To annotate objects or display items in grass, soil or a mud kitchen, attach the items to sticks, using string, a hot glue gun or duct tape, then press the stick into the surface.
- Label everything – see Idea 98, My space, my place.

Bonus idea

Consider relocating your summer term performance to an outdoor area – and hope for fair weather! Outdoor and 'promenade' performances (where the players and audience move around a space) make the most of the outdoor areas you have and will add atmosphere to children's shows – without the need to make 'scenery'! If you're brave, you could even try this for winter shows.

Wrapping and weaving woodland

"A woodland in full color is awesome as a forest fire . . . a single tree is like a dancing tongue of flame . . . " Hal Borland

Whether you have a single tree or a copse — or even just some large shrubs — they can become the structures for large-scale temporary artworks in your setting. Wrapping and weaving trees celebrates the diversity of their unique shapes, sizes and textures.

Teaching tip

A quick start tree web or weaving frame can be created using washing lines or parachute cord (thin, strong rope). Fill in the gaps as and when you have time to source fabric scraps — why not ask parents to donate balls of wool or old sheets and items of clothing that can be torn into strips?

Tree wrapping and weaving is a wonderful collaborative project, with opportunities for personal and social development as children communicate and help one another to manage large scale resources. There is inevitably lots of fine motor skill development too, with fiddly knot tying and problem solving as children manage the manoeuvring of materials around trunks and branches.

Visit scrap stores to find fabrics, cargo netting and wide, robust tapes and use them to weft 'threads' around the 'warp' of the trees. In one setting a copse of about eight trees became a huge weaving frame using rolls of fabric scrap. The resulting web was used for several weeks as an imaginative play environment. After a half term of creative use, the woven materials were cut away and repurposed!

Wrap a single tree trunk (or vertical post) in a variety of fabric scraps, rope, wools etc., focusing on children's descriptive language. Theme a series of tree trunks through the use of colours (complementary/contrasting/rainbow) or textures. Make the most of this as a sorting and choosing activity.

If you lack trees but have large shrubs, it might be possible to shape them. Carefully prune the lower branches to lift the canopy of the shrub and expose the clear trunk below to create a perfect woodland at child scale, ready for weaving and den making.

If you can get hold of long scraps of cargo netting, and have two trees a suitable distance apart, you can include a hammock within your tree weaving. The cargo net itself can be tied and knotted around the trunks – fix it at a low level and check to ensure it is secure before use. This offers another physical challenge as children learn the coordination required to get into and out of a net hammock successfully!

Find out more about artistic tree wrapping: www.christojeanneclaude.net

By Felicity Robinson

Bonus idea ★

If your setting has no trees or vertical structures, consider introducing permanent large scale weaving frames, which can also function as space dividers, providing a level of definition between different activities. These frames are versatile and can also be used for gutter runs or sound walls.

Picture this too

"A giant picture frame can be a magical doorway or even a life-saving raft!"

Creating a huge picture frame from tree branches is a common Forest School activity but serves just as well in a nursery garden. You might want to consider the size of the frame if you don't have a whole forest to work in!

- You will need four long, straight branches. They don't all have to be the same length or diameter, but two similarly-sized long branches and two shorter ones will give you a rectangular frame.
- Choose at least two branches that are slightly longer than your tallest children so that at least one dimension of the frame is bigger than they are and they can walk through it.
- You'll need some thin rope or strong twine and some extra rope or long, double hook-ended bungee cords to secure the frame to a support.
- Using loppers or secateurs, strip the branches of side shoots or small stubs to reduce cut and graze hazards. The branches don't have to be perfectly smooth – the character of the natural material should be evident.
- Lay the branches on the ground and arrange them into the desired shape. Overlap the ends of the branches slightly and then securely connect each corner using a square lash knot – step-by-step instructions for this knot are available online.
- Once all four corners are secure, lift the structure and you have a giant picture frame!

Take a risk!

Part 6

Embrace the mud

"We weren't prepared to get rid of the mud, so we embraced it!"

Having a muddy area in a setting is not always so popular with adults but most children really enjoy it! Managing the mud can be a way of accepting its presence without allowing it to take over the play space. Remember, mud washes off, and children are waterproof!

To embrace the mud, you'll need to manage it and this means several things – children being properly attired, adults being prepared for the subsequent mess and everyone agreeing where it is and isn't okay for mud and its accompanying resources to spread to.

- Examine the mud patches. Which one(s) are you prepared to accept and keep? Consider the mud's proximity to other features such as entrances and exits, pathways and climbing areas. In the right place, mud's slipperiness is part of its appeal; in the wrong place it's a hazard. Consider the size of the mud patch – how many children will want to play in it at any one time? Consider its closeness to complementary activities such as sand and gravel – could these be linked in some way?

- Is it possible to border the mud patch with heavy logs or lengths of timber? These don't need to be permanently installed but should be heavy enough to prevent children from moving them – contact a local tree surgeon for donations. Bordering the patch will limit the amount of mud travelling across the rest of your play space.

- If you have several muddy patches and have now designated one area as the mud patch, ensure children are regularly reminded that the 'old' patches are no longer available for mud play. Reseed them – once children are used to playing in the new 'honeypot' mud patch, the grass has a chance of growing back.

- Make sure children are properly clothed to enjoy mud: readily and independently accessible wellies and waterproofs will make a big difference to parents' attitude to muddy play.
- Agree where mud itself and the mud play equipment (see Idea 22, Mud kitchen) can go – to the sandpit maybe, but not to the shed? Setting ground rules right at the start will help you all enjoy and embrace the mud, by controlling where it can and can't go.
- Storage in or very close to the mud patch will help prevent the spread of mud and its resources across your site. Ensure there are sufficient mud play resources to avoid children having to pilfer from the sandpit or playhouse.

Taking it further

One of the most useful items you'll ever have outdoors is one of the simplest – a water supply. If you don't already have a tap in an accessible position (e.g. near the sandpit, mud kitchen or planting areas) then consider installing one. If that is not possible, a water butt is a great alternative; both offer the potential to enrich mud play – or even enable mud play, in very dry weather.

You learn to fall by falling

"Play is great for children's well-being and development. When planning and providing play opportunities, the goal is not to eliminate risk, but to weigh up the risks and benefits. No child will learn about risk if they are wrapped in cotton wool."
The Health and Safety Executive (yes, really!)

In an increasingly sedentary, risk-averse world, opportunities for children to take risks – physically, emotionally and intellectually – are decreasing at an alarming rate. Your setting is a safe, managed, planned environment and as such is the ideal context for play that is as safe as *necessary* – not as safe as *possible*.

Teaching tip

Your Risk Benefit form can be used to risk assess spaces and places as well as activities.

Whilst children do have an innate survival instinct, they have an equal and opposite desire to take risks. Both of these imperatives need to be nurtured and encouraged – but how can you do this at your setting? The Risk Benefit approach to risk assessment is an appropriate process when considering children's play opportunities. To use Risk Benefit in your setting, simply create a table with five columns:

1. Define the **activity** in question (for example, whittling sticks with a vegetable peeler).
2. Describe the **benefits** children will gain from participating in the activity. Or think of a 'reverse' risk assessment – what would children *miss out on* if they were *not* able to participate?
3. List the **potential hazards** – only do this *after* you've listed the benefits!
4. Explain the **mitigating factors** that will reduce the hazards. The purpose is not to eliminate *all* risk, but to minimise *unnecessary* risk.
5. Decide on the **risk rating** – high, medium or low. High-risk activities can still be undertaken, they just need more planning, more supervision or smaller groups to enable them to happen.

Taking it further

Visit the Health and Safety Executive's website to read their High Level Statement on Children's Play: www.tinyurl.com/ HSEplay. These two pages of common sense guidance will reinforce your understanding of the value of risk in children's play. Jennie Lindon's book *Too Safe for their Own Good* is an excellent introduction to risk-taking in children's play.

Magic wands

"The children really enjoy whittling their very own magic wands!"

Making and decorating magic wands promotes hand-eye coordination, perseverance, attention to detail and care for oneself and others – not to mention the communication and language possibilities as children share their excitement!

'Whittlers' are really just vegetable peelers! A selection of 'Lancashire' peelers (straight ones) and Y-shaped peelers is best as each child will prefer a particular style.

Whittling sticks at your own setting is not difficult, but there are a few basic safety rules to follow:

- Maintain a ratio of around 1:4 for this activity and have a first aid kit handy. Whilst cuts are *not* inevitable, beginners may need more support to get the action right and may graze their fingers occasionally.
- Children should whittle standing up or sitting with knees apart or to one side. A low bench or planting bed/sandpit edge is ideal. Attempting to whittle whilst sitting on the ground is awkward and can lead to accidents.
- Use sharp whittlers – blunt blades will frustrate children and are more likely to cause cuts.
- Always whittle away from the body – and of course away from anybody else's! Ideally, children should whittle between their knees and towards the ground.
- Older, drier sticks are easier to whittle than freshly cut 'green' sticks, so use sticks found on the ground rather than cutting new ones.

The ideal magic wand diameter is at least 1cm – the width of a marker pen – and around 30cm long. Children should whittle the bark off their stick and shape it into a blunt point, then sand it smooth with foam sanding blocks. Decorate wands with marker pens, glitter and acrylic paints and wool.

Teaching tip

If children have not already whittled at Forest School, start them off with long, fresh, crunchy carrots, which are very simple to shave. Make sure the whittlers are clean – then children can eat their whittled carrots as a reward.

Fires in the garden

"Children love to paint what they see in the fire, using big shapes to recreate the sparks and flames."

Safely building, managing and extinguishing a fire is a valuable life skill. Fire building requires patience and children need to understand how to behave around fire and how to keep safe around it. The rewards are rich — cooking, storytelling, singing, science experiments, the smell of woodsmoke in autumn, warming chilly hands or perhaps just gazing into those flickering flames.

Teaching tip

Forest School suppliers Muddy Faces have a free, illustrated guide for teachers and practitioners, *How to light fires safely*. Visit their website at www.muddyfaces.co.uk to download a copy.

Fires can be built in the centre of a simple fireproof container. Locate the container over a hard surface (not grass!) and raise it above the ground using four bricks. You could use:

- a disposable barbecue
- a very large turkey roasting tin or oil change drip tray (unused!)
- a terracotta chiminea — metal versions tend to overheat and are not recommended.

A fire comprises:

- tinder — tiny pieces of flammable material such as newspaper, dry leaves or bark, cotton wool or wood shavings
- kindling — slightly larger pieces of wood such as dry sticks and twigs that you can snap by hand
- fuel — larger pieces of wood, split logs, charcoal or coals.

Teach children to confidently strike a long match, firmly and away from their body, and to quickly but sensibly place the flame against the tinder to light it.

Fires need oxygen to burn, so start by loosely piling the tinder and adding more once it's alight. Then carefully add the kindling in a loose pyramid shape, again adding more as it begins to burn well. Finally, add fuel, smaller pieces first.

Children should not touch the container the fire is burning in, and hair and loose clothing should be tucked away. Keep a bucket of water nearby to extinguish the fire once you are done and ensure your first aid kit contains burn gel and dressings. Other safety equipment could include a fire blanket, heatproof gauntlets and barbecue tools. Make sure the embers are completely extinguished before leaving the fire and do not leave it unattended at any time.

Read on to the following idea (Idea 56) for more fire safety information.

Read on to the following idea (Idea 56)

Bonus idea ★

Why not build a permanent fire circle? The fire pit itself can be as simple as a metre square of bare soil, with large, chunky logs to contain it. The logs will char, but depending on the frequency of fires, will last six months or more before needing to be replaced. Informal log seating will maintain a rustic feel, but you could create a more permanent circular bench seat around your fire pit. Search for 'fire circle design' online, to research ideas.

Making fires safe

"The benefits of enabling our children to build and manage a campfire far outweighed the risks."

If your first reaction to reading Idea 55 and the idea of young children being near a fire is 'no way!' — read on. Building, lighting and extinguishing a fire can be simple, safe and exciting, even with very young children. Careful pre-fire planning will help this to become a regular activity at your setting.

Taking it further

Consider building a permanent fire pit or fire circle. A few hefty logs laid directly onto the ground in a circle to contain the fire itself is a great start. Free standing 'fire woks' and tripods are available from Forest School suppliers online and allow you to start making soup, baking bread or grilling vegetables; search online for 'forest school fire pit' to find specialist Forest School suppliers.

As with any activity, especially those that are higher risk, conduct a Risk Benefit assessment. This focuses on the positive outcomes children will gain as well as the potential hazards and allows you to balance risks and benefits before making a decision about carrying out this activity. The steps below will help you to manage a fire safely:

- To manage the fire you'll need a bucket of water, a gardening glove, barbecue tongs and a stick to use as poker.
- Choose a space that has plenty of room for children to move safely around, is uncovered and away from bushes or other flammable objects. A hard surface or bare soil is better than grass — don't build your fire on bark chips or rubber surfacing!
- Place your bucket of water, poker and fire building materials away from the fire itself, but close enough to grab when needed.
- Place the roasting tin on the four bricks so that it rests above ground level.
- Place the strips of newspaper in the very centre of the tin (only fill the centre with fire). Place the tinder onto the newspaper. Add a few items of kindling to the top of the pile. Ensure air can still circulate in between each level.
- Light the newspaper with a long match. As the fire develops add logs/branches.

Cooking on a stick

"Nothing tastes quite like a sausage cooked on a stick over an open fire!"

Cooking on a fire might seem like an impossible activity in the average setting, but in fact it's eminently achievable and is a safe, exciting, purposeful task that all children can be involved in. With thorough planning, common sense risk assessment and appropriate supervision, cooking on a fire can become a regular activity!

Stress the importance of having clean hands when preparing food, keeping cooked and uncooked meat separate and ensuring food is thoroughly cooked before eating it. Children should take responsibility for their own safety when eating hot food – marshmallows can be meltingly hot and will burn lips, fingers and tongues if children don't wait until they've cooled slightly!

Use food items that cook quickly and won't make children ill if they are slightly overcooked or undercooked.

- Large marshmallows on long, thin whittled sticks (don't be tempted to use kebab skewers – they are too short for children to maintain a safe distance fire and they burn rapidly). This ensures children's hands are kept well away from the fire. To avoid losing marshmallows to the fire, press them right down onto the stick so that its point can be seen.
- Slice a baguette into chunks and press onto the end of the whittled stick (or a toasting fork). Bread toasts very quickly over a hot fire so children should count to ten before turning it over, to be sure it won't burn.

Teaching tip

When cooking over a barbecue, wait until the coals are grey before cooking. Wearing heatproof gloves, remove the grill to allow food on sticks to get closer to the coals. Charcoal doesn't create flames, so if you want them you'll need a wood fire – see Idea 56, Making fires safe.

Taking it further

Search online for campfire recipes – there are thousands! Simple, consistently successful recipes include: drop pancakes, using a flat griddle or paella pan over the fire; damper bread twists on thick sticks or bamboo and vegetable soup, made in a cast iron pot.

Out after dark

"Our children can play outdoors all day, all year round."

Active outdoor play is important at all times and children ought not to be kept indoors just because it's dark — there is much to discover outside at twilight and, with the right resources, it's an adventure children will remember.

Teaching tip

Before allowing children to play out after dark, carry out a risk benefit assessment on the 'dark' playspace — the hazards will be different, although that does not automatically mean more dangerous. You should carry a torch at all times.

Taking it further

Extending outdoor play into darker afternoons or evenings might simply be about installing lighting that enables the space to be used regularly. A mains-connected motion-activated lamp over a doorway (often used to deter intruders) is an excellent and playful way of providing bright light and strong contrasting shadows.

An outdoor play after dark resource box is an invaluable tool in enabling children to make the most of the outdoors all year round.

Focus on children's sensory perceptions, with objects and activities that will encourage them to smell, listen, touch, taste and if they can, see.

- **Smelling:** Put incense sticks and scented candles outside for children to smell, and encourage them to identify what else they can smell: bonfires; strongly fragranced plants, cut grass; local take-aways.
- **Hearing:** Use balls with bells inside and instruments, for example, kazoo, drum, shaker, rainmaker, whistle. Listen for traffic, aeroplanes, church bells or people passing by.
- **Touching:** Get children feeling their way around outdoors, seeking rough/smooth, warm/cold, hard/soft surfaces.
- **Tasting:** Make a small campfire (see Idea 55, Fires in the garden) and toast marshmallows or sausages.
- **Seeing:** Glow in the dark objects such as yoyos and light up frisbees and balls; glow stick bracelets; headtorches and flashlights; solar fairy lights for marking out dens or routes. Get children to chalk out shadows on the ground or use a phone app to identify the International Space Station going overhead.
- **Intuitive perception:** What does it 'feel like' to be outdoors after dark? How is it different from being outdoors in daylight?

Whatever the weather

Part 7

Puddle jumpers!

"There's no such thing as bad weather, just inadequate clothing."

The weather in the UK can be variable to say the least — four seasons in one day is not unusual! But, when properly attired, children and adults can enjoy outdoor play all year round. Children enjoy the experience of rain on their skin, and creating huge splashes in puddles is enormous fun!

Teaching tip

Introduce the water cycle to children by discussing where rain comes from and where puddles disappear to on a warm day.

Involving parents

Build up your welly collection by asking parents to donate wellies once their children have grown out of them. You could also ask for donations of towels so that there's always a ready supply.

Taking it further

Install a water butt under a long length of gutter (the longer the gutter, the greater the volume of water). You will have a free and ever-replenishing supply of water for plants and for sand and water play, and you will be able to create your own puddles on dry days.

Before you begin any of the activities below you should risk assess to 'enable' wet day activities: consider an appropriate group size; how long to stay outdoors; keeping mess indoors to a minimum; and how you'll all get dry again once back indoors.

- Make a double-sided weather sign — with a sun on one side and an umbrella on the other. Explain to children that when they see the umbrella side, it means wear wellies and waterproofs outdoors.
- Invest in waterproof dungarees in a couple of different sizes — dungarees are more adaptable than all-in-ones and will allow children to jump in puddles on warmer days too.
- Draw chalk outlines around the puddles, then jump in them and mark, in a different chalk colour, the extent of the splash. Who can make the biggest splash?
- Brush the water out of the puddles.
- Collect rainwater in water butts to make your own puddles on dry days.

Raindrops keep falling on my head

"Children are amazed that raindrops don't fall on their heads."

Drizzly days are a good excuse to get togged up and let refreshing rain splash onto your face. But exploring rainfall from a different perspective is great fun. This idea shows how, if you invest in a couple of new resources, you can explore a variety of rainy day opportunities.

- Purchase a 'glass clear tarpaulin' (an Internet search using that term will bring up lots of retailers). Expect to pay around £20–£30 for a two metre square tarpaulin. They are manufactured with eyelets so are easy to clip onto fixed points such as trees or guttering.
- Clip up the tarpaulin approximately one metre above ground, and place plastic backed picnic blankets underneath – add cushions or fleece blankets for babies.
- Children lie underneath the tarpaulin, watching the raindrops and rivulets running across and dripping off the edges.
- Place small brightly coloured objects (for example, animals, unifix blocks) on the top of the tarpaulin. Observe how they move and float in the small puddles formed by the rain.
- Ask children to tell you what it feels like under the rain. What shapes can they see in the tiny puddles? Why is the rain dripping from the edges?
- Glass clear tarpaulins are also terrific den building materials, especially when used alongside a camouflage net or tarpaulin.

If your glass clear tarpaulin is big enough, use it for snack time or story time in the rain.

Taking it further

Use the glass clear tarpaulin as a giant canvas – attach it vertically to a wall or fence and provide big brushes and rollers with water-based paint in tubs. Big art is a great aerobic workout and the tarpaulin can be cleaned with washing-up liquid afterwards.

Bonus idea ★

Invest in transparent umbrellas – the main educational suppliers sell them in sets. They can be decorated using permanent marker pens. Play the famous clip from *Singing in the Rain* before going out on a rainy day with your umbrellas to put on your own splashy show.

Ice pendants

"Children love to touch and play with ice. Instead of always telling them to 'be careful' or 'leave it alone', we make the most of icy days to learn about the science of water and the magic of winter."

Invite children to discover the transformation of water into ice (and back again), with this magical winter activity. Ice pendants are simple to make — but require patience — and can be personalised with contrasting or complementary colours or textures.

Involving parents

Make the most of a snap frost by providing parents with instructions for carrying out this activity with their children at home, bringing the frozen pendants into the setting the next day. It's likely that a very diverse range of frozen pendants will arrive, sparking discussion and admiration as they are hung up outdoors.

For this activity, you will need: shallow dishes, for example the lids from plastic food boxes, poached egg dishes or margarine tub lids; cookie cutters; 30cm lengths of string; short lengths of narrow plastic tubing; a jug of water; a selection of attractive objects to freeze in the pendants; a frosty day.

- Before you begin creating your ice pendants, talk to the children about wintry weather and explore what they know about different forms of water (for example, clouds, rain, sea, snow).
- Next, take a walk around the garden, collecting interesting objects to freeze and observing differences in they way the garden looks on a frosty day compared to a spring or summer day. Children's 'found' objects will need to be relatively small in order to freeze securely into the ice; explain that heavier objects might break the delicate ice encasing them.
- Children might choose natural or wintry objects — holly leaves or berries, tiny cones, slivers of bark, shells, pebbles — or they could choose man-made objects such as small world animals, plastic numbers and glitter.
- Arrange the objects in the shallow dishes and place cookie cutters into the dishes to create shaped pendants. To create hanging loops,

either loop the ends of a piece of string into the dish, or place a length of plastic tubing on one end (when removed from the dish this will leave behind a hole in the ice).

- Fill each dish with water. Be careful not to displace the objects and the string/tube. Leave the dishes outdoors overnight.
- The next day, investigate the transformation. If ice hasn't formed, discuss why. If ice has formed, allow children to explore it with their fingers and with magnifying glasses. Ice crystals may be visible, and some of the objects will project from the ice. Some pendants might be more solid than others.
- Hang the pendants from a climbing frame or a tree. If you hang them from your 'transition area' canopy, children will be able to see them slowly melting from indoors. Revisit them throughout the day, noting any changes.

If it isn't quite as cold as you thought outside, it might be necessary to cheat; in which case, quietly place the dishes in the freezer overnight! It's also fun to do this activity in the height of summer, in which case you'll definitely need the freezer.

Taking it further

Collect children's thoughts and impressions throughout the transformation process: what changes did they notice? How long do they think the pendants will last? What environmental conditions might affect the pace of melting? Which pendants lasted the longest? Why? Hang one pendant indoors (over a sink or tray) and observe how long it takes for that one to melt. What can children tell you about why the indoor pendant melts quicker than the outdoor ones?

Watery world

"A simple outdoor tap and a hose pipe transformed our outdoor play."

Access to water is an essential component of continuous provision, and children should have opportunities to experiment with water, indoors and out, every day. An external tap, at a height children can reach independently, is a vital resource – if you don't have one already, make it top of your to do list!

Make water play an easy option by creating watery grab and go resource boxes. Flexible plastic gardening trugs are perfect for storing awkwardly-shaped vessels and tubes. Fill your trugs with:

- Vessels of different sizes to allow filling, pouring, measuring and comparing: dishes, tubs, jugs, differently shaped and sized bottles, buckets, trays.
- Objects to allow experimentation with water flow and pace: funnels, lengths of drainpipe, waterwheels, straws, tubing and pipes, balls of different weights and sizes, glitter.
- Resources that will demonstrate scientific concepts: sponges, solid metal objects, corks, bubble bath, conkers, timber offcuts (for example, balsa, bamboo, oak), ice cubes, pipettes and turkey basters, pumice, food dye, shells.
- Household objects: sieves, ladles, spoons, colander, small pans, measuring spoons, robust weighing scales, slotted spoons, tea strainers, paintbrushes and rollers, exotic fishing nets, scoops.
- Objects that connect water to the other elements and the seasons: conkers, leaves, windmills, watering cans, water sprays, sand and gravel, umbrellas, mud.
- Items that wouldn't ordinarily be used in water play: woollen gloves, cotton wool, magnifying glasses, string, small world people and animals, grapes, mirrors, letters.

Frosty day fun

"Look! Winter fairies have ice-skated all over our windows last night!"

Frost is a beautiful and intriguing phenomenon. Exploring its properties encourages scientific and creative thinking, both of which help children become competent problem solvers. Use the ideas below to seize the opportunity to go outdoors on a frosty day and listen to children talk excitedly about what they find.

- Use magnifying glasses to examine frost crystals up close. What shapes can children see? What colour is frost? What do the crystals remind the children of?
- Choose a few sticks, of varying diameters and lengths, from your stick collection (see Idea 18, Curate a stick collection). Use them to mark make in the frost, testing the different nib widths and discussing (using appropriate language) which length and diameter of stick is most comfortable to use.
- Photograph frosty leaves, spiders' webs, and even car windows and bonnets, which often have stunning frost patterns. Use the images to inspire frost paintings indoors – mix silver glitter with white paint to create frosty sparkles. The marbling technique can also create shapes and patterns that mimic frost.
- Frost makes fascinating displays all over the garden – take a tour to find the most abstract/biggest/smallest. Can children see any similarities between the shapes and patterns?
- How quickly does frost defrost? Choose a heavily-frosted area and revisit it every half an hour on a sunny day. What do children notice about how the frost is melting? What happens if children breathe onto frosty surfaces – and why?

Bonus idea ★

Another vital element to explore on an icy day is children's balance and coordination. Allow them to walk on the ice, testing their ability to stay upright. They will need to concentrate to learn how to move (slowly, with deliberation) and how to regain stability if they slip. Learning how to negotiate icy surfaces in the safe, managed environment of your setting will enable them to cope with slippery surfaces in the 'real' world.

Snow school

"Snowy days are often our most enjoyable and collaborative days."

Staying indoors on a snowy day is a missed opportunity. With the right clothing and careful pre-planning, you can afford to be spontaneous. Time outdoors in the snow will be memorable — just make sure there are warm drinks available to defrost everyone afterwards!

Teaching tip

At the beginning of winter, write to parents to tell them that you plan to play out in the snow, and request that children are sent to the setting in warm layered clothing and stout shoes or boots. Keep wet weather gear in an accessible place so that children can play outdoors.

Bonus idea ★

Always remember to photograph these ephemeral snow artworks! Laminate and display the photographs outdoors to help children recall what they made. Consider including photographs of the children completing their snowy artworks, in the outdoor gallery.

Children's toes and fingers will become cold quite quickly in the snow, so several short periods outdoors may be better than one longer session.

Useful equipment for snowy days includes:

- Vessels of varying sizes — buckets, trugs, measuring jugs, food containers and yoghurt pots are great for making snow bricks for igloos.
- Watering cans, water squirters, turkey basters and buckets can be used to bring warm water outdoors.
- Gardening and sand play resources such as spades, bottles, sieves and funnels.

Snow school activities:

- Encourage children to sweep up routes through the snow to their favourite play spaces. Sweeping is an excellent aerobic activity and will warm up children quickly.
- Use sticks (see Idea 18, Curate a stick collection) to mark make. Practise making shapes, angles and arrows with sticks.
- Use the snow from the sweeping activity and offer found objects such as cones, leaves, twigs and bark chips to extend the concepts.
- Make snow portraits. Give children mirrors so they can see their own faces, and demonstrate how they can mould the snow to recreate the contours of a face. Use your found objects to fill in facial features such as hair and eyes.

Snow art

"...snow is exhilarating; there is really no such thing as bad weather, only different kinds of good weather." John Ruskin

Few things are quite as compelling to a child as a blanket of pristine, untouched snow. Try to keep everyone off fresh snowfall until you are ready to make your snow art pictures. This ephemeral art will only last for a limited period, so make the most of the snowy canvas to make giant pictures!

Collect natural materials to create the artworks – have these in reserve so you are ready for a suitably snowy day. Working outdoors means the children's art can be enormous, so choose big objects, or an abundance of smaller ones. Consider collecting or identifying sources of the following:

- straight and curved branches and twigs, with or without leaves
- conkers, cones and nuts
- pebbles and stones, slate and gravel
- charcoal from your fire (see Idea 56, Making fires safe)
- leaves – beech leaves are particularly beautiful all year round
- moss or lichen
- dried grass cuttings or hay
- mud

Use the snow itself – roll it into balls or fashion trenches or hillocks. Most environmental art celebrates the materials and the landscape rather than representing a literal subject. Allow children to be inspired by the materials they are handling and encourage them to search for and talk about patterns, shapes, colours and textures in the resources they have.

Remember to take photographs of the finished pieces!

Teaching tip

Show children examples of work by artists who use natural materials and an ephemeral approach. Artists such as Martin Hill and Andy Goldsworthy are inspired by the seasons and by colours, textures and shapes in the natural world.

Whatever the weather grab and go box

"Children are happy to be outdoors in any kind of weather if they are appropriately dressed."

Although grab and go resource boxes are now very popular in educational catalogues, they're rather costly, and won't necessarily contain the items your children will most enjoy using. Curating your own resource boxes is a great ongoing project, and the contents can change from year to year, depending on the fascinations of your children.

The purpose of the grab and go box is to allow scientific experimentation and stimulate language skills outdoors. Pose lots of open-ended questions, for example, 'What happens if . . . ?' 'Where will it go . . . ?' 'Why did it do that?' 'How can we change it?' Use the resources for different types of weather, for example, on a windy day in different places around the garden. The effects of a blustery day will be different to a breezy one, and children can examine the difference between sheltered and exposed spots outdoors.

The contents of a whatever the weather grab and go box might include:

- Windsocks, windmills and spinners
- Bottles of bubbles
- Handheld anemometers (or weather vanes) to check the wind direction and speed
- Garden thermometer
- Feathers, ribbons and streamers
- A short handled fishing net
- A few beach buckets
- Water sprayers (for example, plant demisters)
- Two large cotton sheets, one with four or five 1cm slits cut into it
- Plastic bags, cotton reels and string to make mini parachutes.

Shadow chasers

"This is a simple way to show how the earth spins and moves around the sun."

Use this activity to demonstrate a number of tricky concepts, such as the passage of time, the movement of the Earth around the sun and on its own axis, and temperature changes throughout the day. These may seem like complicated concepts for pre-schoolers, but many children will enjoy practical experiments like this one.

- At the start of the day, choose a hard surfaced part of the garden for this experiment. You'll need a space with a deep shadow.
- Ask children to chalk along the outline of the shadow in a particular colour, and somewhere along the shadow line write the time.
- Continue to do this every hour (or half hour) throughout the day, using a different colour of chalk each time. Touch the ground or play space features that are in full shade and full sun – what do children notice about the temperature? What do children notice about the chalk shadow lines as the day progresses? Are there some places that are no longer in shadow at all? Where do they think the next shadow line will be made? Sometimes we see the sun and the Moon in the sky at the same time – why does that happen? Ask children to think about how dark it must be on the other side of the world if there is no sun or Moon in their sky.

Teaching tip

Take photographs of the chalk lines during the day – later, project them onto a whiteboard or wall as a time lapse set of images so that you can discuss what takes place as the sun moves across the sky.

Taking it further

Borrow a globe to show children the Earth moving on its own axis. Darken the room and use a torch to represent the sun to show children that as the Earth moves on its own axis, parts of the world go into shadow and night falls.

Scientists and engineers

Part 8

Dens and hidey-holes

"Children use creative and descriptive language as they collaborate to build a den."

Teamwork is essential in order to build on a grand scale, and problem-solving is inherent, for example, establishing how one item can join on to another! Use a den building session as an opportunity to question children about their thinking, encourage gross and fine motor skills and foster imaginative and collaborative play.

A den building kit is an early years setting essential and is not necessarily an expensive resource. Your own bespoke kit will be far cheaper than any ready-made set and will offer far more play value, so allocate an initial budget and make your own. Remember to replenish the kit regularly, paying particular attention to the supply of 'joiners' (see below) and wash the fabric elements every so often.

For your den building kit you will need:

- A small tarpaulin with eyelets (pound shop or DIY store)
- Plenty of sheets and blankets (charity shop, jumble sale, parental donations)
- Plastic shower curtain (pound shop, parental donation)
- LOTS of 'joiners': plastic and wooden pegs – including 'dolly' style – string, bungee cords, shower curtain rings and clips, bag clips, short lengths of rope – bulldog clips, large chunky elastic bands (market stall, DIY store, pound shop)
- Carpet tiles and samples (carpet shop)
- Cargo netting (parental donation, scrap store)
- Parachute with loops (educational supplier, toyshop)
- Tent pegs and plastic tarpaulin pegs (camping store, pound shop)
- For adult use only: scissors, cable ties, secateurs and longer lengths of rope.

Stargazers

"They are so excited to see the Space Station whizz over their heads!"

During the winter months, darkness falls early and on a clear evening it's possible to stargaze from your setting — even in an urban setting. Have books, apps and resources to help you quickly identify what children can see. The Internet has made stargazing much easier for the amateur.

Children's attention spans will be limited at the end of the day, therefore it's vital that you plan ahead so that (weather permitting) you know there will be objects of interest to observe on the night.

Find out when the International Space Station (ISS) will pass overhead at a suitable time using an app such as ISS Tracker, NASA or Satellites. Once you've chosen a date and time, use a Planisphere (available from bookshops), or the Pocket Universe app (or other astronomy app) to establish what else will be visible. Look out for the constellations that are bright and can easily be described to children, for example, Cassiopeia, the Plough and Orion, whose belt is particularly easy to spot.

Satellites move quickly and directly through the sky without blinking, unlike aeroplanes. The ISS is fast, very bright and unmistakeable. Aim to be all settled outdoors a couple of minutes before it is due to pass overhead, to allow children's eyes to adjust to the darkness. If there is lots of light pollution, advise them to shield their eyes with their hands and focus on one spot in the night sky.

There is also a live feed from the ISS on the NASA website – www.nasa.gov and incredible pictures of deep space taken by the Hubble Space Telescope – www.hubblesite.org.

Teaching tip

Children should be warmly dressed and you should plan to stay out no longer than five minutes when you first start stargazing. As children become more familiar with the constellations they will be willing to stay outdoors longer – but an early experience with cold ground, cloudy skies and frozen fingers is likely to put them off.

Taking it further

The Facebook and Twitter feeds of Col. Chris Hadfield are a rich source of information about life on board the ISS and even though he's now retired, he continues to link to current space missions.

The cardboard rocket

"This rocket idea is a perfect incentive for imaginative play outdoors."

Rockets require a lot of cardboard – ask parents or a local electrical appliance retailer to donate large cardboard boxes. Encourage children to participate as much as possible in the rocket's construction.

Teaching tip

Introduce this activity by showing children footage of rocket launches, space walks and experiments on the International Space Station (ISS). The NASA website (www.nasa. gov) includes archive and recent footage, as well as live launches that occasionally might happen at the right time of day to watch with the children.

Alongside cardboard, you'll also need several rolls of strong duct tape, sharp scissors and a sharp craft knife, white emulsion paint, paintbrushes or rollers and marker pens, plus glue and objects for decoration.

Sketch a drawing of the rocket first, with approximate dimensions. Make sure the finished diameter of the rocket will be big enough to allow several children to get inside – 5m of cardboard will create a rocket just over 1.5m in diameter. The height should be at least 2m, since approximately 50cm of that height will be trimmed to make the nose cone.

It's easiest to create the rocket flat then roll it up into a tube, so first separate a few long pieces of cardboard for the 'fins' and then join the remaining pieces of cardboard together using strong duct tape – you may need to tape the seams on the inside and the outside of the rocket. Cut the rocket to the desired dimensions (for example, 2m x 5m).

Mark out features such as portholes and a doorway and cut them out with scissors or a craft knife. Cut out two or three long, thin fins from the leftover cardboard and attach them to the body of the rocket by cutting tabs along the long length of each fin and taping them alternately left and right for rigidity.

To make a pointed nose cone, cut out deep triangles from the top of the rocket, so that they look rather like the points on a tall crown. When the rocket is rolled up, these can be taped together to make a cone.

Roll up the rocket and tape it and the nose cone elements securely along the seams.

Paint the exterior (and interior if you like) with a couple of coats of white emulsion paint, then mark on the features of a rocket – lights, flags, lettering etc. Children could use mosaic techniques to do this, or glue on coloured paper, bottle tops and foil food trays to represent buttons and solar panels. To make a shiny silver rocket, purchase foil blankets (the type athletes use to keep themselves warm) and glue them to the rocket's exterior. Foil blankets can be purchased in pound shops, usually in packets of two, so are far more cost effective than rolls of tinfoil.

Involving parents

At home, parents and children could make papier mâché planets using round balloons. Ask them to paint their planets in different colours and once dry, thoroughly cover them in PVA glue. The glue will dry clear, and will afford the planets a tiny bit of outdoor longevity, so that they can be suspended from trees, pergolas or canopies to add to the space theme across the garden.

Bonus idea ★

Many of the experiments on the ISS involve exploring how solids and liquids behave in zero gravity or a vacuum. Why not encourage your young chemists and physicists to explore the properties of materials by setting up a space station lab in your mud kitchen (see Idea 22, Mud kitchen)? Introduce clear plastic and shiny stainless steel vessels and implements, droppers (for example, turkey baster), bashers (for example, meat tenderiser), rolling pins, coloured water and facemasks to help children get into character. Inspire children to test the properties of rock, water, mud, chunks of natural chalk, flint, tree bark, grass and any other natural material you can find. You could also ask them to wear washing-up or gardening gloves, and perhaps goggles too, to find out how difficult it is to be accurate and precise when wearing a spacesuit!

Rocket science

"We can't use fireworks on Bonfire Night so we make rockets during the day!"

Set up a rocket science lab outdoors and have fun with pops, bangs and explosions! This idea provides a simple idea for demonstrating Newton's third law (every action has an equal and opposite reaction) to your pre-schoolers. Or, you could just do them because they are great fun!

Teaching tip

Use the Risk Benefit approach to ensure you carry these activities out safely. These explosion activities are adult led; the materials and equipment can be hazardous and they are designed for children to enjoy watching, not setting up. Other issues to consider include keeping a safe distance from the explosions; storing the vinegar and bicarbonate of soda separately; ensuring there is sufficient vertical and horizontal space to allow the rockets to launch without hitting windows, trees or people and keeping sharp knives, valves and needles out of children's reach.

To make a water rocket, you'll need one-litre or two-litre plastic drinks bottles, a foot pump with a football valve adaptor, a cork, a metal skewer (or long mattress needle) and a garden fork.

- Shape the cork with a craft knife so that it will fit snugly in the neck of the bottle.
- Make a hole through the length of the cork using the skewer or mattress needle and insert the football inflation valve through the hole, ensuring the end of it protrudes beyond the cork.
- Pour water into the bottle until it's around 1/3 full, and insert the cork in the neck.
- Push the garden fork into the ground at an angle of around 30–45 degrees. This is your launch pad.
- Attach the foot pump to the football inflation valve and arrange the bottle upside down in the handle of the fork so that it stays put, with the valve and cork pointing downwards through the spade's handle.
- Pump like mad – children will be able to see air bubbling into the bottle and when the pressure becomes too great, the bottle will shoot off its launch pad into the air, leaving the valve and cork behind.

To make a vinegar rocket, you'll need a 35mm film canister or similar lidded small container (not the 'click-lock' type), a bottle of vinegar, a tub of bicarbonate of soda, kitchen roll and a spoon.

- Carefully pour a small amount of vinegar into the bottom of the canister, taking care not to get any on the insides.
- Hold a small square of kitchen paper over the opening of the canister, pressing it gently down so that it makes a 'well' – the paper mustn't touch the vinegar.
- Place a teaspoonful of bicarbonate of soda onto the kitchen paper and replace the canister lid, trapping the kitchen paper and bicarbonate of soda in place, away from the vinegar.
- Quickly turn the canister onto its lid – and move away!
- As the vinegar mixes with the bicarbonate of soda, the reaction creates a gas that builds pressure in the canister, which will suddenly shoot up into the air leaving a frothy white mess behind.
- If you can set up several vinegar rockets and have space to safely turn them over one by one, it makes a very impressive (and funny) display.

Bonus idea ★

Before jet propulsion was invented, missiles (for example, flying objects) were launched using a variety of methods. Invent your own Heath Robinson style launchers, beginning with a simple slingshot – a long length of wide elastic tied between two sturdy posts or trees. Pull back the elastic as far as it will go, place an object (a small pine cone, wool pompom or soft toy, for example) into the elastic and release! Safety first: make sure your flying object won't fly through a window or into someone's face. Arrange the slingshot so that the objects land in an open space – that way, you can measure the distance and height achieved by different objects (or different sizes of the same object).

Giant jigsaw

"I never thought of making a puzzle out of our actual garden!"

How well do your children know your site? This treasure hunt type activity uses life-size photographs of parts of the features in your garden to enable the children to discover the space. It's a great way of helping new children familiarise themselves with the space and persuading 'old hands' to see it with fresh eyes.

- Take lots of close up photographs of permanent features in your garden – for example, parts of the climbing frame, the sandpit, an outdoor tap, trees and shrubs, fences. Choose examples that can be seen every day, so avoid pictures of wheely toys, hollow blocks or flowers as these could be in different places from day to day – or of course, not be there at all.
- Choosing just *parts* of each feature or object (for example, just the corner of a sign or the lock mechanism on a gate), print them in colour on A4 or A5 at as close to real life scale as you can. To do this, place a piece of A4/A5 paper against the real object, photograph that too and then crop the original image to match the chosen paper size.
- Trim and laminate each photograph to symbolise a piece of a jigsaw. Make several sets of jigsaw pieces, joining them together using string or a key ring.
- Give out the jigsaw sets to each child or pair of children. Can they find the original feature or object?

Taking it further

See the complementary activities Idea 73, Giant jigsaw 2 and Idea 76, Shape hunt.

Giant jigsaw 2

"Children are fascinated by the changing seasons and keen to explore outdoors in almost any kind of weather."

Record the passage of time with high-resolution photographs you can enlarge and laminate to allow children to compare and contrast the view throughout the year. This simple jigsaw activity stimulates plenty of discussion about contrasts and similarities as well as helping children speculate about what will happen next. It also encourages big body movements as they sort through the pieces.

It will take you a year to get this activity fully up and running – but it's worth it! On the same day every month and at a point during the day when children are all elsewhere, take a landscape photograph encompassing as much of your garden as possible. Try to include plant material, permanent features and moveable objects such as bikes and trikes. Kneel down when you take the photograph so that the garden is captured from a child's eye view – and be sure to choose a location that they can easily access when they come to carry out the activity. Enlarge each month's photograph so that it will take several sheets of A4 to complete the whole image – for example, two sheets tall by three sheets wide. Print each piece of the image in colour on A4 and laminate it. Use a permanent marker to record the month on each piece of jigsaw.

- Sitting in the same position you were in when you took the photograph, can children put all the pieces together to recreate the view?
- Once you have sets of puzzles from several months and seasons, ask the children what they notice about the puzzle view and the real view. Changes between January and February might be quite subtle – look for shadows, first buds and cloud formations. The differences between January and July are likely to be much more obvious.

Teaching tip

Make the jigsaws more demanding by cutting up the laminated pieces into random shapes – two or three to each A4 sheet, making a 36 piece puzzle rather than a 12 piece puzzle – remember to label each piece with the appropriate month.

Taking it further

Look for signs of time passing in the first and last puzzles you made – for example, plant growth, number of pictures pinned to the fence, volume of sand in the sandpit!

Tarp-tastic top ten

"I would be lost without our 'glass clear' tarp!"

Tarpaulins are cost-effective, adaptable and invaluable. Invest in several tarpaulins of different sizes and finishes and keep them in a dedicated box along with a selection of 'connectors' so that they are always ready for use. It's important that children can use most, if not all of the connectors, as manipulating connectors is an excellent way of developing strength and dexterity in children's fingers, hands and arms.

Involving parents

If you have a large grassy space, ask parents to lend their tents for a few days. Once children have thoroughly explored making their own dens, introduce two or three real tents, ranging in size from a pop-up festival style tent through to a large family tent. Children will love helping to erect – and then of course playing in – tents.

Den building is one of the most enduring play activities; few children (or, indeed, adults) can resist the lure of fabric, tarpaulins and pegs. A selection of tarpaulins and connectors means you are always ready to make the most of the opportunities den building offers for collaboration, problem-solving and communication. Pound shops sell small tarpaulins – 1m square, but it's also worth investing in a couple of bigger tarpaulins, especially a glass clear one. Spend as much as you can afford so that the tarpaulin has heavy-duty borders and eyelets in order to maximise its longevity.

Below are ten top ideas for what to do with your tarpaulins!

1. Practical connectors include bungee cords, string, clothes pegs, shower curtain rings, elastic hairbands, short lengths of rope and tent pegs. Choose brightly coloured connectors – they are easier to find when they end up buried under leaf litter!
2. Lay a tarpaulin under a tree and shake the tree so it catches anything that falls down – in autumn, collect leaves or cones; in spring collect blossom.
3. Use a tarpaulin to create instant shade where it's needed. Attach it to trees or climbing equipment, or use A frames or washing lines to give it structure.

4. Build dens with tarpaulins – children can use the connectors and sticks to shape their own special places. Camouflage tarpaulins are terrific for den building in bushes and trees.

5. Hang a glass clear tarpaulin horizontally just above children's head height on a rainy day so that they have a giant screen under which they can watch raindrops fall (see Idea 60, Rain drops keep falling on my head).

6. Make an instant paddling pool by building a low containing wall with hollow blocks (or logs) and arranging the tarpaulin over the top. Fill the pool with water and then tuck the ends of the tarpaulin under the blocks to avoid trip hazards.

7. A glass clear tarpaulin hung horizontally, or laid flat on the ground, makes an excellent dry wipe marker canvas – a huge one, which will encourage children to really express themselves on a grand scale. You can also use water-based paints on the tarpaulin.

8. Create a cosy story space by arranging cushions and blankets over the top of a tarpaulin and providing baskets of books. Tarpaulins are much bigger than picnic blankets so allow several children to lounge around, sharing books together.

9. Lay out all the connectors on the ground – ask children to attach all of them to the tarpaulin. Can they make repeating patterns of connector type (for example, peg bungee string, peg bungee string) or colour patterns?

10. Weave a long length of rope or string through the tarpaulin's eyelets, and draw it together, making an enormous parachute or bag but leaving a 'cave' entrance. Place collections of objects inside the bag to allow children to explore them inside the cave.

Taking it further

Some den builders may be curious about using real knots; the Scouts' website has an excellent, illustrated PDF download showing several simple knots, which more dextrous pre-schoolers can try: tinyurl.com/simple-knots. Apps are also available for tablets, with knot-tying videoclips.

Geocaching

"It was so exciting to find a geocache hidden in our local park!"

Geocaching is a form of scavenger hunt that makes the most of today's GPS and smartphone technology — participants play hide and seek with miniature canisters, sometimes containing a tiny piece of 'treasure' or a minute scroll of paper contating the names of finders. Use the Geocaching.com website or app, or invent your own trail in your play space.

Taking it further

If you can find a large-scale map of your locality, mark the locations of known geocaches using the website or app. If you make a trail in your own play space, draw a sketch plan of the site and mark on your geocaches. Remember to include a north point and a scale on your plans.

Find out where your nearest geocache is by inputting your setting's postcode into the geocaching.com website. Geocaches are graded in terms of how difficult they are to find, but there will be at least one nearby that you could try to find with a small group of children.

You can also make and hide your own geocache and upload its details to the website for others to find. If you hide it on the external boundary of your site, seekers will be able to find it without disturbing the setting and you will be able to check it regularly to see how often it's been found.

Typical geocache containers include 35mm film tubs, small ziplock bags and fake pebbles. Choose a hiding place that's well out of sight of casual passers-by, for example, tucked inside a gap in a tree trunk or attached to the rear of a fence post with elastic bands. When you record its details on the geocache website, you can add a clue to help geocachers find your treasure. Discuss what the clue could be with the children.

Playing out counts

Part 9

Shape hunt

"The competitive element of this shape hunt really appealed to our children!"

Support children's understanding of the variety and complexity of shapes in the real world by setting a task to find every example of each shape, outdoors. The tally chart aspect will work for some children; others will choose alternative ways to record their results.

Include common shapes such as circles, squares, rectangles/oblongs, ovals, different types of triangle, semi-circles in your shape hunt. Make sure there are at least a few easily identifiable examples of all the shapes you include. Add one or two shapes that require more perseverance to find, such as a star.

- Make a worksheet to attach to a clipboard, with an example of simple shapes on the left hand side and space for mark making on the right. Depending on the child, you could ask them to indicate a number, make a tally chart or draw what they see and then tell you where they saw it.
- Provide children with a cut out cardboard shape, big enough to hold comfortably in their hand. A piece of chunky chalk will help them mark out each example they see. Tour the garden with the child to count the examples they found.
- Offer children a set of laminated cards with shape words on – around a dozen very common shapes and three or four less common ones. Give each child a blob of sticky tack and ask the group to find shapes that match the words. They should then attach each card to a corresponding shape using the sticky tack.

Beanbag maths

"I'm keen to find ways to make maths memorable and purposeful for our young children. Using physical movements helps children recall their numbers and they love the challenge of beanbag maths."

Reinforce number concepts with simple beanbag games outdoors. This activity can be adapted to suit any space and any age or number of children. Focus on using mathematical language throughout – talking about the *weight* and *colour* of beanbags, the *number* and *size* of buckets, and so on.

Collect a range of different sized vessels, ideally of different shapes and colours, for example, buckets, large yoghurt or food pots, click-lock plastic tubs, plastic or metal vases, a traffic cone on its side. Arrange each item in its own space and give each one a number by chalking on the paving adjacent to it.

Use a broad permanent marker to write a number from 0–9 on one side of a beanbag. On the other side, indicate the same number using dots – choose different coloured beanbags and ensure you have at least ten beanbags so that each digit from 0–9 is represented. Draw a chalk line on the ground. Children will stand behind this line to throw their beanbags towards the collection of vessels.

Taking turns, children should aim their beanbag at the vessels. For younger children, use this idea for colour matching – aim to match the colour of the beanbag with a similarly coloured vessel . For older and more able children, they should attempt to get their numbered beanbag into the appropriately numbered vessel.

Teaching tip

To add an element of competition, pair children up to see who can get the most beanbags into the vessels, or count up the total number of points gained through accurate throwing.

Taking it further

Giant inflatable dice add a new dimension to outdoor maths. Throw one or two dice to find out which vessel to aim the beanbags at. Since the total on two dice will add up to a maximum of 12, this is a good way for more able children to begin to demonstrate their understanding of numbers beyond 10 and even to introduce simple number bonds.

Bonus idea ★

Provide clipboards, paper and pencils to allow children to make tally charts showing their success (or otherwise) in correctly aiming beanbags into the vessels.

Height charts

"Distance is a tricky concept for young children given they are growing so quickly themselves!"

Exploit the special nature of the outdoors by creating a range of height and distance indicators throughout the space and providing children with the means to make their own marks on the charts.

- On a wire or ball-stop fence, cut up coloured plastic bags into ribbons, and using a marker pen, write each child's name onto one end of a ribbon. Measure children's height and write the corresponding figure on the other end of the ribbon. Tie the plastic ribbons along the fence at the appropriate heights.
- On vertical surfaces such as gateposts, doors or play equipment, use acrylic paint marker pens (also known as Deco pens) to write children's heights.
- On horizontal surfaces, paint distances onto the ground, using playground paint. Begin at the gate into the garden, or by the main door used to exit the building. For example, paint 10cm from the start, then 25cm, 50cm, 1m, 5m, 10m etc. Give children a metre ruler and a bag of chalk to allow them to mark interim distances.
- For metre marking, use exterior paint or acrylic markers to indicate metre distances in various places around the garden. Regularly seeing 1m markers as they play will help children recall and estimate this distance, later assisting their understanding of fractions and multiples of a metre.

20:20

"When we thought about taking number learning outdoors, a whole new set of ideas emerged."

Develop children's understanding of the numbers one to 20 with these simple, active outdoor ideas. Hands-on learning is highly effective for most young children and the physical movement elements will help them with recall. These ideas work equally well with numbers one to 10.

- Give children a matchbox (a large matchbox is best) and ask them to collect 20 tiny natural objects, to store inside it, for example, seeds, gravel, leaves. Make the task trickier by giving children a smaller matchbox.
- Choose a month during which children will be at the setting for 20 days or more – spring or autumn are best for this activity. Tour the garden and agree on a feature that might change over the course of 20 days, for example, a tree losing its leaves or produce appearing in a vegetable garden. Discuss how and why it might change. Provide a camera so that children can take a photo of the plant/fruit every day for 20 days. Print out the photos and ask children to place them in chronological order. What changes can they see? Why did they happen? What might happen in another 20 days?
- Chalk the numbers one to 20 onto the paving. Make it trickier by placing the numbers randomly around the space. Ask children to find, and call out, each number in order, or in reverse, or pick out specific numbers (for example, the child's age).

Taking it further

Extend the matchbox idea by spreading out everyone's found objects onto a blanket or tarpaulin. Can the objects be grouped (for example, leaves together, tiny cones together)? Which objects were collected most frequently? Who collected the biggest/ smallest object? What colour are most of the objects? How many objects are there in total?

Bonus idea ★

Why not introduce these activities using numbers one to 20 in a different language? If you have children with English as an additional language, use the languages they use at home, to help everybody become fluent in them. Young children are remarkably adept at picking up languages – try Spanish or French too.

Maths grab and go box

"In this 'real world' task, children develop their mathematical language."

A maths 'grab and go' box is a handy resource and can be used in many ways – not just for maths activities. Imaginative play and language skills can both benefit from the introduction of measuring tools and a few dressing up items.

Your maths grab and go resource box should contain:

- A trundle wheel
- 30cm ruler
- 1m rule
- A retractable 2m sewing tape measure
- A retractable 10m builders' tape
- A set of wooden callipers – some designs allow a piece of chalk to be attached to one 'leg' of the callipers for drawing circles with
- Sheets of squared paper and pencils
- A couple of clipboards
- Unifix cubes

Talk to children about comparing and estimating distances – is it further to the gate or further to the slide?

Examine the measuring tools. Which of them would children use to measure a long distance (for example, the whole length of the garden or the height of the slide)? Which would they use to measure a small distance?

Encourage the use of mathematical language such as higher than, lower than, longer than, in between, half of, shorter than and above.

How long is a piece of string?

"As an early introduction to mathematical ideas of perimeter and area, this string activity helps children understand that the edges of objects are often much longer than the object is itself."

Introduce new mathematical language through measuring objects children find outdoors. They'll enjoy the challenge of creating the longest piece of string. Also, manipulating the string and cutting it with scissors will improve their hand-eye coordination and manual dexterity.

This activity works best with groups of up to six children. You'll need several small balls of string and pairs of children's scissors.

Discuss with the children the length of an object and its perimeter – a large, irregular-shaped leaf is a good example. Do they think the edge of the leaf is longer than its length or width? How do they know?

Demonstrate the measuring technique by holding the free end of the ball of string at the base of the leaf, then following the leaf edge with the string until it meets the beginning of the string. Cut the string at this point. Before lifting the string to see how long it is, ask children to hold their hands apart to show you how long they think the string will be. Did any children guess correctly?

Give each child in the group a ball of string and some scissors and ask them to find something they'd like to measure the perimeter of using the string. It doesn't have to be a living thing – it could be the perimeter of the sandpit, or around a fence post.

Teaching tip

Don't throw away the strings – put them in the maths grab and go box or a den building box so they can be reused.

Bonus idea ★

Show the children a picture of Leonardo da Vinci's Vitruvian Man drawing, which aligns the human body with a square and a circle. Ask the children to lie on the playground in a similar pose, and draw around their silhouettes with chalk. Each child uses their ball of string to establish whether they can make a square or a circle from their outline – but don't cut the string. Use it to measure the perimeter of their body outline, this time cutting it so that they can compare the length of their string with those of other children.

Mad measuring

"When I was a child I measured everything in 'Uncle Phillips' – two metres to be precise."

Do you still think about how many 'bags of sugar' something weighs? Calculating in tangible units can be the first step in understanding measurement, so this activity, which uses an 'average' sized child as the unit, will cement the idea of distance being measured in multiples (or fractions) of units.

This activity works best with a big group. Ask the children to organise themselves into a straight line with the shortest child at one end and the tallest at the other. Discuss how they are working out the correct order, and what they'll do if two or more children are exactly the same size.

Each child should stretch out their arms to their sides and touch the fingertips of the adjacent children. The child in the middle is the median (average) height – halfway between the tallest and shortest child – and becomes your 'non standard unit'. Let's call this person 'Rachel'. Ask the other children to look at Rachel and her outstretched arms, so they can judge what one 'Rachel' looks like (the distance between her fingertips).

Now guess distances in Rachels, for example, 'How many Rachels will it take to get from the gate to the sandpit?' Rachel is your 'average' so you can then use all of the children, fingertip to fingertip, to measure the distance. Some children's arm spans will be smaller than a Rachel and some will be greater, but it will average out.

Taking it further

Is measuring in 'Rachels' a good idea? What units do we now use to measure with? What other measuring units can children find on their bodies? For example, foot, handspan, elbow to fingertip.

Bonus idea ★

Leonardo da Vinci's Vitruvian Man drawing was based on the work of Roman architect Vitruvius, who lived in the 1st century BC. Vitruvius thought that the 'perfectly proportioned' human body was eight heads high. Are the children's bodies eight heads high? Why not? In fact, young children's heads are proportionally larger than adults' heads and the smaller the child, the fewer 'heads' high they will be. If you allow the children to measure you, it's likely your height will be close to that 'perfect proportion'!

How many beans is this leaf?

"This simple way of introducing the mathematical concept of area also helps children understand what different quantities look like."

As children become more confident with their counting skills, encourage them to start thinking about how they apply this knowledge.

You'll need a big bag of dried beans for this activity.

- Collect several leaves from the same tree – different sizes are fine.
- Ask children to lay the leaves out on the ground, smallest to largest. Talk about how they are making these size choices. Some leaves might be longer or wider than others, so how will children decide the correct order?
- Give each child a leaf and get them to draw around the perimeter of their leaf with chalk, then cover it with kidney beans, hiding as much of the leaf's surface as possible without going over its edge, and placing the beans flat, not overlapping. Can children guess how many beans they needed to cover their leaf?
- Beginning with the smallest leaf, take the beans off one by one, counting as you go. Chalk the number of beans needed for each leaf onto the ground adjacent to the leaf's outline.
- Repeat the exercise, this time with leaves from different trees and talking about the different shapes and sizes of leaves you have in the garden. What other objects could children use to measure the area of a leaf?

Teaching tip

Introduce or reinforce mathematical language such as bigger than, widest, compare, outline/perimeter and area. Ask children to think about fractions, for example, half a leaf.

Taking it further

Ask children to measure the leaf area using unifix cubes or a bagful of cut up squares from centimetre-squared paper. How many whole units do they need? How many parts (or fractions) of units? Use measuring tools from your maths grab and go box (see Idea 80) to experiment with other ways of measuring length, width and area.

Bonus idea

Plant runner beans in pots, and when they've finished flowering use the beans in the pods to measure the area of a runner bean leaf. Then save the beans to plant next year!

Spider's web numbers

"I love the hand-eye coordination and concentration this demands!"

This is a simple idea that requires minimal resources. You can make it more complex if you like, but the purpose is the same: to encourage children to think and act quickly and to recall (or recognise) number patterns. It also works as a simple phonics exercise. Fewer children in the group makes it simpler, more makes it trickier.

- Stand the group in a circle and give each child a number, starting with you as number one and moving clockwise around the circle. If it's a small group, or a more able one, ask children to remember their number and everyone else's. Otherwise, chalk large numbers onto the ground or stick a small number card onto each child's clothing so that everyone can see it.
- Hold the end of the string in one hand, and the ball in the other. Call out a number, and throw the ball of string to that child, who must catch it and repeat the action. The catcher keeps hold of the piece of string they caught and throws the ball of string away. Catching and throwing whilst holding a piece of string in the other hand is not easy!
- Continue until each child has had a catch and throw at least twice. By now you'll have a great spidery web of string and the string ball will have been dropped several times.
- Ask the children what they notice about the pattern they've made? How can they untangle the web? Was it hard to catch and throw?

Treasure island

"We love to imagine our garden as a treasure island, full of hidden treasure!"

This treasure hunt game makes the most of children's curiosity and builds on their knowledge of familiar features in the outdoor space by introducing geographical and mathematical skills. The preparation to set up the treasure island ready for play is really worth the effort – once you've created an annotated plan, it will be reused often.

To make treasure maps, start by creating an A3 plan of your garden. Indicate the boundary as a shoreline, include a north point and rename the features in the garden to give them pirate connotations, for example, the sandpit could become 'Captain's Cove'. Photocopy the original plan and then squeeze a used teabag onto the reverse of each copy, squishing it around, to create the impression of ancient parchment. Once the maps are dry, laminate them.

Hide a piece of treasure in the garden and chalk a large X somewhere on the ground. Mark the X on each laminated map using a dry-wipe marker and set children off to search for the treasure. They should count their steps from the X to the nearest feature and mark the map to show their route.

Give the children mathematical clues to help them find the treasure, using words such as 'behind you', 'nearby', 'under' and 'next to' to help them identify its location. You could also suggest they walk a specified number of steps (for example, five, or 20) in a specified direction (for example, 'towards Captain's Cove').

Taking it further

Enhance the treasure island theme by sharing story books, dressing up as pirates or singing sea shanties and chants. Create emergency shipwreck shelters using your den building kit (see Idea 68, Dens and hidey-holes). Add a physical challenge by fashioning eye patches so that they negotiate the treasure island using just one eye!

Up and at 'em

Part 10

Newspaper snowball fight

"This activity was mayhem indoors. Outdoors, the children thought it was hilarious."

This madcap throwing game is a marvellous whole body physical activity, requiring flexibility and speed. Precise targeting isn't vital to the game, so it's great for younger children who are learning how to throw accurately. What's more, as each group has to stay within its own base, children can be very physically active without needing huge amounts of space.

Teaching tip

Make this trickier by reducing the size of the bases. This makes it more likely that the newspaper snowballs will miss their target, so children need to be more accurate. You could also insist that they can only throw one snowball at a time – good luck enforcing that!

Bonus idea ★

In winter, play the game for real, making sure participating children have waterproof gloves. Make a big stash of snowballs for each base and set the timer for a short period. Avoid cheating by playing the game on an area of paving that's been cleared of snow, so that sneaky children can't make extra snowballs to throw!

This game works well with up to 20 children.

- Use a hosepipe, chalk or sticks to mark out a very large circle on the paving or grass and then mark that out into four quarters, or bases.
- Divide the children up into four groups and allocate each group a base of their own.
- Give each group of children a couple of broadsheet newspapers and get them to separate the pages and screw them up into 'snowballs'.
- Once they have a stash of snowballs, the aim of the game is to throw as many as possible into the other three groups' bases. Of course, the other three groups will be throwing snowballs into *your* base, so they must be thrown back too.
- Set a timer – a minute is plenty for younger children but older children will keep going for five minutes or more.
- The winning group is the group with least number of snowballs in their base when the timer alarm sounds. Snowballs that have fallen beyond the boundary don't count to the group's score.

Tail tag

"Perfect for children who need to be physically active throughout the day."

Tag-style games are sometimes undervalued but are great for children's physical agility. In order to succeed at tail tag you need speed, balance, hand-eye co-ordination and the ability to change direction quickly. This is a boisterous loud game that children love!

All you need for tail tag is a large outdoor space and a collection of brightly coloured fabric strips, approximately 10cm wide and of varying lengths – the 'tails' should not drag on the floor as they'll become a trip hazard, so choose lengths that will allow children to play safely. Tails are made by simply cutting or tearing an old sheet into strips. Choose a bright colour so that the tails can easily be seen in play.

Each child should tuck a 'tail' into their waistband. If they don't have a waistband, tie a length of wide elastic around their waist. The object of the game is to grab as many tails as possible in the time allowed and put them in your own waistband, whilst protecting your own tail(s) from thieves. The winner is the child with the most tails when the alarm goes off.

The number of children participating will depend on the size of space you have – in smaller settings children may have to take turns. Decide ahead of time how many rounds and set boundaries.

Teaching tip

The lack of physical contact (only the tails are grabbed) enables children who struggle with touch to enjoy participating in an active group game.

Balloon bend and balance

"Balloons are tricky to control outdoors. That's why we love them!"

Test children's agility, balance and co-ordination with games that use balloons of various sizes and shapes. There are opportunities to add other areas of learning to the games to make the most of colours, shapes and numbers. Balloons are much lighter and forgiving than balls, so perfect for younger and smaller children.

Collect balloons of varying shapes and sizes, from tiny water balloons to large latex balloons. Play the following games to encourage children to throw and catch, balance, hit, pass and bounce balloons:

- Stand children in a circle, and use half as many balloons as you have children. Children must pass the balloons across the circle by batting them with their hands, keeping as many of the balloons in the air as they can for one minute. Balloons that fall on the ground should be removed.
- Make a huge pile of coloured balloons. Children take one balloon at a time, and find an object in the garden with a similar colour.
- Mark out a short track using a chalk or rope line. Give each child a balloon and ask them to hold them between their ankles, knees or thighs. They attempt to jump the length of the track, without losing the balloon.
- Use balloons for warm up activities outdoors. Children hold a small balloon in one hand, or a larger one in two hands, to aid balance and co-ordination when performing arm and torso stretches.

Marching matters!

"Let's march!"

Marching is a simple and effective way to get children moving with meaning. You cannot march without putting some effort into the action. Ideally, you use your whole body to move with purpose around your garden (and it's fun too!). What's more, singing and chanting rhymes can really help language development and adding this to movement makes it even more fun.

Children love to march – they also like to hear nursery rhymes adapted for them and their own setting.

- Choose a rhyme that the children know, such as *The Grand old Duke of York* or *This old man*, (also known as the *Children's marching song*), and sing along together as you and the children march around the garden.
- Dress up or play musical instruments (of any kind!) as you go, and beat out the rhythm as you march.
- Adapt the words of the rhyme to suit the circumstances of your setting and your children, for example, 'The children of St John's, they marched along the path / they marched right up to the big tall tree / and they marched back down to me'. It really doesn't matter if it doesn't rhyme!
- Try old marching rhymes too, making sure you step out on the correct foot as it is emphasised in the italicised words, for example, 'He had a good home but he *left*, (right), *left* (right), *left* / Since then he's never been *right*, (left), *right*, (left), *right*'.
- Find more marching tunes by searching online: www.songsforteaching.com has song lyrics.

By Mary Jackson

Teaching tip

Encourage children to lift their knees up high and pump their arms backwards and forwards as they march. They could also turn their heads as they go around corners, taking care not to move their shoulders! Marching should be a whole body activity that gets everyone moving (including you!).

Taking it further

Taking a walk beyond your site can be a great way to motivate children into walking further, or to move a little faster as you head home. Using rhymes and songs will help keep them going even longer!

Tricky terrain

"Unfortunately, the 'real world' isn't carpeted in rubber tiles!"

Children learn new skills at a phenomenal rate. They advance from lying to rolling, crawling, cruising, walking and running in just a few years. However, their constantly altering centre of gravity presents a challenge, one that you can help them manage by offering unusual opportunities to test their balance, agility and coordination.

Outdoors is the perfect place for physical development activities, such as those below, offering space to move and air to open the lungs and get the blood flowing.

- Set out on a backwards trail: children stand back-to-back, holding hands and attempt to walk along a chalk or rope line.
- Use hollow blocks, crates and logs to build a safe route through crocodile infested waters.
- Use gymnastic techniques (see Idea 91, Playground parkour) to encourage children's agility and coordination.
- On a soft surface such as grass or sand, strike the yoga pose known as the 'Cat' (on hands and knees with back arched) and try to move around the space as smoothly as possible.
- Float like a butterfly, sting like a bee: copy the movements of animals and insects – galloping, slithering, flapping.
- Line children up one behind the other, each holding one corner of a floaty scarf. The leader should plot a route around the garden, visiting various features and moving at a pace all participants can match.

Playground parkour

"Parkour feels subversive, and all children feel a frisson of joy at that!"

Parkour (or 'free running') is a high-energy urban sport, that makes use of the features and fixtures in the built environment as gymnastic equipment. It's an exciting, risky activity, but can be adapted for all ages and abilities. The playground or garden makes a perfect first parkour course for small children and appeals to their innate sense of adventure and mischief.

You'll need to do a Risk Benefit assessment of the suitability of your outside features for parkour moves before children have a go at it (see Idea 2, Planning safe outdoor play), and ensure they are wearing sturdy shoes. Bumps and scrapes are inevitable – even the professionals get injured – so be ready with kind words and a first aid kit!

Plan parkour for a specific time and explain to children that this is a special activity; this idea is not about allowing children to use the playground features for parkour *all the time*. A bench is just a bench when it's not parkour time.

Show YouTube clips of professional free runners and discuss the concept with the group.

Tour the garden as a group, pointing out features that could be used – children should think about bouncing, stretching, leaping, swinging, balancing, running and jumping. Practise these movements on the features of your garden.

Once children are comfortable with parkour moves on individual features, the trick is to join the moves together by sprinting between features to create a flowing, joyful, agile circuit of the garden. They'll need to watch out for fixed and moving obstacles including other free runners!

Teaching tip

Develop this activity in stages in order to build on and build up children's confidence. Climbing up the playframe is not the same as jumping from it – sitting on a bench is not like free running along it or rebounding from it. Allow children to go at their own pace and provide encouragement so that they graduate to higher, faster or trickier moves.

Taking it further

Once your children become competent at leaping, bounding, climbing and rolling around your own garden, offer them the open spaces of the local park or playground, which will incorporate the added challenges of larger, more challenging obstacles such as people, bicycles, pushchairs and dogs.

Slopes and slides

"Music is the universal language of mankind." – Henry Wadsworth Longfellow

Using sounds to complement movement helps children develop their understanding and use of language as well as encouraging how they move around your outside space.

Use musical sounds to help describe actions or activities that children take part in outside. Observe the children going up, along and down slopes, steps, climbing equipment and pathways. Walk alongside them, 'accompanying' them as they move up, down or along by intoning descriptive words as they move.

For example:

- As children go up a slope you might sing 'going up, going up, going up, going up' – raising the pitch of your voice each time as they also rise upwards.
- If they are jumping from log to log, you might sing, 'Juu-uummp!Juu-uummp!' changing the pitch of your voice for the take-off and landing.
- If they are going down a slide, scoop your voice down in a big 'Wheeeeee' – starting up high and ending down low as they slide to the bottom.
- On the bikes and trikes, intone 'pedal pedal pedal pedal' in a rhythmic pattern, slowing down and speeding up to match the child's pace.

By Mary Jackson

Capture the flag

"The combination of excitement, physical activity and sneakiness really appeals to our older pre-schoolers."

This activity works well in a big outdoor space as it's a very physically active game. Two teams try to capture one another's flag, without being tagged and sent to the opponents' jail.

If you don't have flags, take two lengths of fabric, in different colours, and tie each one to a stick, broom handle or length of bamboo, or hang over a tree branch.

Divide the group into two teams. If you're playing in the park, you could have quite large teams. In your own setting, three or four per side is plenty as this is a very physically active game.

Each team should mark out a 'jail' in their own territory, for tagged opponents – a hula hoop or skipping rope works well for this, or even a sandpit or willow tunnel.

One or two children on each team should stay to 'guard' their own flag, the others are tasked with capturing the opponents' flag. Whilst doing that, they need to try to tag the opponents, thereby sending them to jail and of course, avoid being tagged themselves.

Jailed players can be released by being tagged by a member of their own team.

The winners are the first team to capture their opponents' flag and bring it back to their own territory.

Teaching tip

Your role as an adult is to act as referee, making sure tagged children go to 'jail' in a timely manner and ensuring that in all the excitement, tagging remains a gentle gesture.

Bonus idea

Why not make your own pennants? Fold a large square of brightly coloured fabric in half to make a rectangle. Cut a V shape into one of the shorter sides and then sew the three 'open' sides up using a zigzag stitch to reduce fraying. Finally, sew four lengths of ribbon onto the short, straight side. Use these to tie the pennant onto a chunky stick the height of a child.

Speak out

Part 11

Take a line for a walk

"Straight lines go too quickly to appreciate the pleasures of the journey." – René Crevel

Whatever the size of your outdoor space there will be room to take a line for a walk. This idea involves exploration at different scales, setting challenges, or even just contemplating. It can give you and the children a new perspective on your own, very familiar, outdoor learning environment.

A line can be a versatile device to encourage specific learning outcomes. Set up a 'line' around your outdoor space, using resources appropriate to the scale of the task:

- Chalk lines leading to a series of physical challenges across a large space, or a length of knitting wool to take a child on a minibeast safari around a single shrub.
- A hosepipe or heavy mooring rope can be a robust line to follow through a woodland area or large shrubbery.
- Lines can be made of modular resources as well, or even sand.
- Use trundle wheels to navigate along a line, ask children to practise counting each click as they roll along.
- Take a line around the site with cards tied to it at relevant points. Each card might suggest an observation, or you could set up something exciting to discover at each point.
- Trust walks can use lines set up around the outdoor space, with one child leading another, blindfolded, to experience textures scents and sounds.

By Felicity Robinson

Story stones

"A personal and powerful way of developing storytelling skills."

Story stones can be used outside in all weathers, all year round and will add a splash of literacy into any zone. By involving children in the creation of a collection, they make a personal connection to the environment and the story stones have greater meaning to them.

Begin by reading a story such as *Everybody Needs a Rock* by Byrd Baylor. This provides useful guidelines for finding good rocks, for example, a rock has to feel just right in your hand, and it has to smell good.

- Show children one or two stones that you have found. Talk about where rocks may be found locally and what is okay to pick up. Encourage the children to hunt outside. Dig for rocks in the garden, visit a local green space, or ask parents to search with their children.
- Thoroughly wash gathered stones and decorate them using acrylic paint markers. Children have to decide what the design represents and this will vary with each storytelling session.

At story time, let the children create their own story, using the story stones as inspiration. Begin with a character, perhaps a soft toy. As each child holds the toy, they decide what happens next in the story based upon their stone, for example, a stone with white marks may represent a snowstorm. Once a child has made their contribution, they add their stone to the growing line of pebbles.

By Juliet Robertson

Teaching tip

Keep repeating the story as each child contributes, so they can recall the story's progress and look at the stones placed in order. This activity needs several sessions to help children develop their storytelling abilities. Begin by modelling a short example to show the children how to participate.

Taking it further

Build up collections relating to specific themes and interests, for example, have a sparkly set of stones for use in role play. Stones can also be painted with letters of the alphabet, words and numbers.

Laminated story books

"Our laminated books can be read wherever children feel like reading."

Don't throw out battered books — the pages may be a little dog-eared, but by laminating the pages you can provide children's best-loved books with a whole new lease of life outdoors. If you have multiple copies of books, use one of each for this task. Alternatively, visit market stalls, library sales and charity shops — and it doesn't matter if they're not in perfect condition.

To create your laminated story books, use a craft knife to carefully slice the pages apart from the binding, and trim tatty edges (or to fit your laminating machine). Leave a good wide laminated border, and punch holes around the perimeter.

Here are a few ideas for using the books:

- Rebuild the story book by joining the pages in the correct order using treasury tags, key ring split rings or lacing a ribbon through the punched holes. Children can then enjoy the story wherever they are outdoors.
- Mix up the pages and ask children to put them back together in the correct order, retelling the story as they go.
- Suspend individual pages around the garden (for example, water tap, slide, shed door) and give a small group of children a piece of chalk each. Their task is to seek all the pages, and then retrieve them in the correct order, marking each page location with a chalk numeral, beginning with '1' for the first page of the story.
- Give each child a page from the same story and encourage them to act out what they see (or can read) on their page. Use locations around the garden to add interest and character. Can children make a play of the whole story by acting out each 'scene' in order?

Sign of the times

"Children suddenly noticed new words all around them."

Words and sounds are all around us. Send children on a language treasure hunt around the grounds or garden and open their eyes to the language that shapes and informs our everyday life.

In this fun idea, children are challenged to use just a portion of a piece of text to work out where the original text is located!

- Take photographs of every piece of writing you can find in the setting's grounds – noticeboards, signs, road markings, fire hydrants, inspection covers, posters. Print out each picture and trim it in such a way that only *part* of the image can be seen – or upload the pictures to your computer and crop the images before printing.
- Laminate each image separately then punch a hole in the corner of the laminated border of each image and bundle together half a dozen or more, using a treasury tag.
- Give pairs of children a set of cards, and ask them to tour the garden, identifying the full text using the partial text they have.
- At each location children should discuss what the text means and what clues they used to find the correct location using just their cropped picture.

Taking it further

Source a large plan of your site (for example, an architect's drawing or a Google Earth satellite picture) and help children to identify the location of each piece of text on the aerial view. Encourage them to find very familiar features – roads, trees, gates – so that they can begin to understand their route and therefore the locations of their 'treasure text'.

Bonus idea ★

For more able children, print and laminate simple phonic sounds, which you know can be found outdoors, and ask children to find objects outdoors that include those sounds. For example, a card with 'ee' – search for a tree or a bee; a card with 'ch' could be a chair or a bench.

My space, my place

"This encouraged our reluctant mark makers to 'tell' us what they thought."

Research suggests that children read messages and meanings in the outdoor spaces they occupy. Indoors, the environment is controlled by adults. This is clear to children from the height of displays through to the out of bounds areas. Outdoors, the space and many of the features are child-sized and can be manipulated to meet their requirements.

Teaching tip

Leave the labels out for as long as the marks made on them can be seen. Children often return to their labels to add new information, or will be inspired to label other places and objects, often with increasingly sophisticated symbols.

Taking it further

For more able children, combine mark making about the features outdoors with a mapping exercise, where children attempt to locate each labelled area on an aerial view of the garden. This activity sends very clear messages about the spaces children value and want preserved and the spaces that need improvement.

Find out more about the places and spaces children value by asking them to label them.

- Create 100 laminated labels in the shape of an old-fashioned parcel tag – you can make four from one sheet of A4 paper.
- Provide children with a dry wipe marker and a set of ten labels each.
- Tour the garden with the group, asking open-ended questions about how each area is used, what children like/dislike about the spaces and features and encouraging them to extend their vocabulary in describing these spaces.
- Once the tour is over, ask children to revisit places of interest around the garden and to leave a label marked with a word, symbol or image to articulate how they feel about the space. For example, a place children enjoy using could be marked with a small picture of the sun, a tick, a smiley face or even words.
- Carry a small collection of pegs and sticky tack with you – string or elastic bands won't be suitable for every place or object children choose to label.
- Later, revisit the labels with individual children, encouraging them to talk to you about the marks they made and what they mean. You may wish to annotate the reverse of the label to aid interpreting and assessing children's mark making.

Painted pebbles

"The children find the process of decorating the pebbles as enjoyable as using them afterwards."

Cobbles and beach pebbles are wonderfully tactile objects – it's hard to resist handling them to feel their cool, smooth surface or to compare the weight of two pebbles, one in each hand. An absorbing collection of painted pebbles offers alternative ways to familiarise children with numbers, letters, symbols and phonic graphemes.

Deco pens are permanent markers filled with weatherproof acrylic paint and are the simplest and least messy way to paint pebbles. Whilst not cheap, they will last a while if used carefully and their trump card is the ability to create accurate and precise marks. Permanent markers will work on pebbles but the colours won't be as vibrant or long-lasting. Using a different colour for each set of pebbles helps children distinguish between them when searching through for a particular symbol, shape or number.

- Use a single colour to paint a letter of the alphabet on each pebble – you could differentiate between consonants and vowels by highlighting or underlining vowels. Mark several pebbles with common letters so that children are able to create words.
- Use a different colour to produce a set with simple cc and vv phonic graphemes, for example th, sh, oo, ee and ai.
- Write several sets of numbers on another set of pebbles in yet another colour.
- Symbols such as mathematical functions, punctuation marks and any symbols you use to highlight text or tasks in the classroom could also be painted onto pebbles.

Teaching tip

A collection of pebbles will be heavy – don't allow children to carry the container and take care not to overfill it. Leave the pebbles outdoors, perhaps on the periphery of your sandpit, or adjacent to a mud kitchen so they are continuously available. Talk to the children about playing appropriately with pebbles – for example, do not throw them or abandon or bury them in the playspace.

Taking it further

Not every child is interested in or able to sit still indoors. Encourage physical movement whilst using the pebbles – sorting by size or weight, ordering by value, matching colours, and labelling objects around the garden with the first letter of their name.

Mini-me story starters

"Children think it's so funny to find their photo hidden in a bush!"

Inspire storytelling and imaginative play scenarios by placing laminated photographs of children and objects around the garden.

Take full-length photos of children, some alone and others in pairs or threes. Print the pictures in full colour onto A4 paper – you should be able to fit two rows of photographs on a sheet so that each 'child' is around 12cm high. Cut these out and laminate each photo, taking care to make sure there is a wide laminated border around each one to prevent water ingress.

Hide the laminated photos around the garden. To hide them in bushes, tape them to a stick and push the stick into the ground so it looks like the mini figures are standing up unaided. On a hard surface, glue or sticky tack the laminated photos. To suspend the figures from trees or pergolas or to attach them to a fence, punch holes in the laminated borders and use short lengths of string or cable ties.

Children will use the figures in all sorts of ways – they'll enjoy just finding them initially, but they work well as the stimulus for storytelling. Before beginning a story tour, ensure the 'key participants' are in place; if laminated figures have been left in the garden, they are likely to have been transported to other places, which could affect the route and outcome of the planned story.

- Start by reminding children that stories generally have a beginning, a dilemma, a solution and an ending.
- Ask children to explain how the mini-me came to be in this curious location: 'How on earth did tiny-you end up behind that shed, Kaashif?'

- Walk around the whole garden, adding to the story each time you find a new mini-me: 'Aha! When you looked under this tree, you found Tiny Brianna – what did you both do next?'
- Enrich the stories by placing unexpected objects next to the mini-me figures – for example, a large plastic dinosaur, a ball of wool, a tea strainer, a similarly sized doll or teddy bear – these could become prompts for the story dilemma or solution.
- To help children independently find laminated characters in a particular order, chalk arrows on the ground.

Remember to take photos of the children leading their stories, and reflect with them once the story is over. Ask children to recall what happened in their story, who was involved, what the dilemma was and how the story ended.

Taking it further

Change the locations of the laminated figures every now and then and restart the storytelling. You could also laminate mini pictures of famous people, such as the Queen, the nursery or school Head or a TV celebrity, and explore what they might be doing in the garden.

Further reading

If the ideas in this book have inspired you to explore outdoor play in more detail, there are plenty of exciting and accessible resources available in libraries, bookshops and online.

Theory and good practice

- Rethinking Childhood is the blog site of the author, play innovator and advocate of rich, diverse and risky childhoods, Tim Gill. Tim comments on the media's obsession with health and safety and his challenges to this have helped shape attitudes to risk in play across the UK and beyond. His writing is engaging and lively and details of his books, including the influential *No Fear: Growing Up in a Risk Averse Society* can be found on the website: www.rethinkingchildhood.com
- Jan White has spent a lifetime playing, thinking about play and sharing her immense knowledge of play in the early years. Her work includes books, articles, training DVDs and projects to help settings make better use of what they have outdoors. Her blog site is crammed with articles, commentary and advice, plus links to her book *Playing and Learning Outdoors:* janwhitenaturalplay.wordpress.com
- *Exercising Muscles and Mind* by Marjorie Ouvry highlights the likely connections between movement and young children's neurological development. She makes a strong case for lots of outdoor, active play, particularly for boys, and a good companion volume is *Too Safe for Their Own Good* by Jennie Lindon which looks at the importance of risk and challenge in childhood.
- Over the past twenty years, Helen Bilton's work has influenced the way we think about outdoor play in the UK. Her approach has always been child-centred and she's a charismatic speaker – her seminal book *Outdoor Learning in the Early Years* (now in a third edition) is a good place to start.
- In *The Coombes Approach: Learning through an experiential and outdoor curriculum*, ex-Heads of the school Susan Rowe and Susan Humphries delight in sharing the ebb and flow of their truly innovative school, across the seasons and across many years.
- Teacher Tom is a pre-school leader at an American pre-school. His blog and Facebook page are witty, generously illustrated, thought-provoking and hugely popular: teachertomsblog.blogspot.co.uk

Explore risk and challenge in outdoor play

- *Managing Risk in Play Provision* is a collaborative booklet published by Play England which can be downloaded as a PDF from www.playengland.org.uk.
- The full text of the *Shared vision and values for outdoor play in the early years* (see Idea 1) can be found here: http://tinyurl.com/visionvalues
- Read and download a PDF of the Health and Safety Executive's High Level Statement on the importance of a balanced approach to risk and challenge in children's play (see Idea 53): http://tinyurl.com/HSEplay
- Explore the unique work of author and 'tinkerer' Gever Tulley who promotes the idea of children engaging in 'dangerous' activities: www.fiftydangerousthings.com. The activities are, of course, safe and risk assessed – and some of them are adapted in this book (see Part 6: Take a risk!).

Innovation, ideas and prompts

Facebook and Twitter are fantastic places to find others just as passionate about outdoor play as you are. Hundreds of practitioners share ideas and innovations from across the globe, on their own pages or within discussion groups. Browse these as a starting point:

- **Learning for Life:** engaging blogger Kierna Corr shares the daily routines of her nursery class in Northern Ireland. Their outdoor space isn't huge, but they certainly make the most of what they have: www.facebook.com/nosuchthingasbadweather
- **Let the Children Play:** Australian Jenny Kable shares ideas, best practice and answers queries from around the world: www.letthechildrenplay.net
- **Creative Star Learning:** ex-headteacher Juliet Robertson's comprehensive and generous website includes activity ideas, blog posts and downloadable resources: www.creativestarlearning.co.uk
- **Free-Range Kids:** author Lenore Skenazy has long campaigned for children to experience a more natural, risk embracing, self-reliant childhood. Her common sense blog is readable and often includes suggestions for getting outdoors: www.freerangekids.com
- **Love Outdoor Play:** the Play England campaign to improve access to outdoor play for children of all ages: www.loveoutdoorplay.net
- **Highway Farm:** read this blog and you'll wish you were four again. Martin and Jane lovingly but truthfully report the adventures of Highway Farm's pre-school children; their enticing outdoor environment is the envy of the many visiting practitioners they host: www.highwayfarm.com

- **Forest School:** if you're interested in learning more about Forest School and how its principles can shape your everyday practice, the Facebook 'Forest School Discussion Group' is a lively place to begin.

Specialist support to develop your outdoor space

www.playlearninglife.org.uk – specialists in early years and primary curriculum development; inventive landscape design for early childhood settings focusing on natural materials, open-ended resources and cost effective solutions to playspace transformation; outdoor play and curriculum focused CPD and mentoring for teachers and practitioners.

www.ltl.org.uk – the national school grounds and early years outdoor play charity, offering hundreds of free online learning resources, national programmes for schools and settings and funding advice.

www.outdoormatters.co.uk – Gail Ryder Richardson's extensive experience of supporting early years outdoors includes stints as an inspector and with the National Strategies. Her creative but pragmatic approach has helped hundreds of settings transform their approach to outdoor play.

Other references and further reading included throughout the book

Idea 6: Gibson, J.J. (1977). 'The Theory of Affordances' in R. Shaw & J. Bransford (eds.). *Perceiving, Acting, and Knowing: Toward an Ecological Psychology. Hillsdale*, NJ: Lawrence Erlbaum.

Nicholson, S. (1972) 'The Theory of Loose Parts: An important principle for design methodology *Studies in Design Education Craft and Technology* Vol 4.

Idea 17: www.sunsmart.org.uk and www.sunsmart.com.au

Idea 18: Danks, F. and Schofield, J. (2012), *The Stick Book: Loads of things you can make with a stick*. London: Frances Lincoln Ltd.

Integrating sticks into the curriculum: www.creativestarlearning.co.uk

Idea 22: Jan White's Mud kitchen booklet is available to download from Muddy Faces, www.muddyfaces.co.uk

Idea 32: *Hapa Zome* printing: www.kindlingplayandtraining.blogpot.co.uk and artist India Flint's website: www.indiaflint.com

Idea 34: Common Ground website: www.commonground.org

Idea 40: Cloud appreciation society: www.cloudappreciationsociety.org.uk

Idea 44: Wild Sanctuary: www.wildsanctuary.com

Idea 52: More information on tree wrapping: www.christojeanneclaude.net

Idea 69: International Space Station feed: www.nasa.gov

Pictures from the Hubble Telescope: www.hubblesite.org

Idea 89: Song lyric site: www.songsforteaching.com